# FUNCTIONAL TRAINING

## BUILD • CONNECT • PERFORM

ROSS YOUNG MSc

THE CROWOOD PRESS

First published in 2019 by
The Crowood Press Ltd
Ramsbury, Marlborough
Wiltshire SN8 2HR


**www.crowood.com**

**British Library Cataloguing-in-Publication Data**
A catalogue record for this book is available from the British Library.

ISBN 978 1 78500 579 4

**Dedication**
This book is dedicated to my amazing wife and kids who believe in and inspire me to be better today than yesterday; to Eileen and Pam, incredibly important women in my life, loving and supportive, taken too soon; and finally to anyone who was told 'you'll never amount to much' ... prove to yourself, you can.

Typeset by Jean Cussons Typesetting, Diss, Norfolk

Printed and bound in India by Replika Press Pvt Ltd

# CONTENTS

# CHAPTER 1

# PRINCIPLES AND FOUNDATIONS

## What Do we Mean by 'Functional'?

To be functional is to be useful, to have purpose, to be well designed. How applicable is the solution to the challenge in front? This does not necessarily mean does this replicate, mirror or tick every box of the criteria, so much as does the solution provide enough to make an improvement or performance enhancement to a situation?

An alternative definition of function may be more applicable to human performance and is defined as 'an activity that is natural to or the purpose of a person or thing'. Therefore being functional could be seen as having a special activity, purpose, or task, i.e. a functional role.

Function could therefore be described in terms of training and movement as the performance of activities to purposefully enhance the natural movement ability of the person in order for their movement expression in competition to be improved.

How is functionality measured? We critique. We identify specific items of the action, process and/or performance, to identify the most important components. In the workplace or business world this may be in the form of targets sometimes referred to as Key Performance Indicators (KPIs), which again break down the role of the person or team and the performance of that unit. In any case, they are checklists, specific figures or targets that need to be met in order for a performance increase to occur.

In sport and fitness, we will also identify areas key to success within a given challenge. Within team sports we ask questions such as have the athletes added to the overall performance of the team, the competition? Have the athletes been a useful asset? Were their performances purposeful or wasted?

Was their game plan well designed? These types of questions are being asked of the athletes periodically. They are often answered through performance indicators. For example, did the athlete get bigger, faster and/or stronger? We can quantify these with changes in body weight, specific speed over a set distance comparison, or via endurance or strength testing protocols for comparison of the result pre and post training or competition.

In the field of performance enhancement, the coach must be critical of him or herself in the same way, and especially critical about their chosen methods, or philosophy. The coach's role is to enhance performance on the field, court or pitch. Therefore the training schedule must be **useful** to the athletes, it must have a **purpose**, a reason for performing and not be there to fill time in the daily schedule. This all culminates in is it **well designed**? Does it do what is required (or more than) for the athlete to perform at the optimal level for the individual?

Often coaches can get sidetracked by new ideas or buzz words and lose themselves.

After years of interacting with many sports coaches, trainers and professionals, it is overwhelmingly obvious that the simple basics work fantastically well and will always work. There are no short cuts that last.

These ideas and buzzwords have been used within the fitness world to enhance the appeal of a trainer's methods and or philosophies. Throughout the past twenty-five years a number of these buzz words have come and gone as the thing to be seen to be advocating at any one time; they include core stability, instability training, tabata intervals, sport-specific, threshold, fartlek and non-specific fitness. The phrase 'functional training' seems to have been hovering for a long time, waiting for its chance in the spotlight though not really enjoying as much time spent in understanding it as other methods. This is likely the reason why many athletes, coaches and parents have possibly mislabelled functional training, or been misinformed as to what it really means, and have followed the route of sport-specific training, often too early in an athlete's career.

Sport-specific training encompasses repetition of the main movements within the sport. Take the sport of rowing, for example. Traditional training views are that the athlete must become more efficient at the movement sequence of rowing, and the way to do that is repetition. I have personally seen hundreds of athletes being 'educated' by their coaches post-race that the way to get the first place is by doing more miles than the winners, and that they will be upping their training on the water and on the rowing ergometer. In that view the rower who at the point of competition has performed the most strokes should in theory win. However, this is not necessarily the case. To illustrate this, Helen Glover became a world silver medallist just three years after taking up the sport of rowing following a talent identification programme in the UK.

It is this misguided view that could also be damaging the next generation of athletes. As the information on training is becoming ever more readily available through the internet, parents and coaches are finding increasing numbers of supporters of sport-specific training, who are pushing this idea onto other coaches and athletes in the hope that getting the '10,000 hours' practice required to become a master of a skill or sport will produce the next sporting superstar. This focus on a single sport from a young age, which in the industry is called early specialization, often leads to the early drop out of the sport by those who don't make the grade quick enough.

Functional training is arguably the reverse of sport-specific training. It generalizes across sports and identifies common themes of movement in relation to orientation, loading and the true muscle action. These components take us a step closer to understanding the term functional training.

Looking at movements and applying what you know about those movements to an athlete in his or her discipline allows you to use a less restrictive training approach. Typical actions you see in land sports involve sprinting, jumping, rotational striking and moving from side to side. So surely we can identify that training movements to enhance these general sport actions can enhance a player's performance. To improve a rugby centre's speed over the first 10m will be similar to improving a high jumper's speed during the approach and similar to a soccer goalkeeper getting off his line to a through ball. The end result may be different but the methods to achieve the desired outcome are comparable.

Functional training therefore looks to enhance primarily the sport's general skills rather than performing only specific exercises to enhance a specific sporting action. That is not to say sport-specific drills and actions are excluded but a holistic movement approach is taken that should allow sport-specific movements under its umbrella.

## The Mechanical Gym Problem

By looking at how we play sports we can identify weaknesses within modern gym technologies and why some training tools are more beneficial to the functional athlete's training programme.

With a few exceptions, the following statements are true for many sports:

- Sports are played in upright positions on your feet, though the amount of time that both the athlete's feet are in contact with the ground is low
- Sporting environments are dynamic; there are forces outside of the athlete's control that will influence performance and movement
- Sporting movements encompass the whole body in motion.

Most modern gyms in our towns and cities are now well equipped with machines for every muscle group; most of these machines allow for simple understanding of the cause and effect nature of training. Look at the pec deck or chest press. This machine will help you build a bigger chest because the muscles used in the action are the pectorals. No doubt the constant pounding of the machine will give you a bigger chest, as performing endless leg extensions will give you bulging quadriceps, and preacher curls provide you with T-shirt-gripping biceps. But answer this, in modern popular sport, where has the biggest bench been the difference in winning and losing a rugby, soccer or hockey match? Or where has having the highest numbers on the leg exten-

sion given a tennis player an ability to place a drop shot?

The answer: they haven't. Where the exercise involves sitting or lying and moving a single joint in isolation there is little function and the exercise is placed low on the functional continuum.

If the exercises we perform are within the remit of a sport's general action, then we can more effectively train a useful component of the athlete's game. Therefore, the more functional exercises we can incorporate into our training the better results we will have. Not only that, but the better our time will be spent. Exercises that challenge not only our relative strength, but our coordination and balance will have a greater benefit to the dynamic component of sport.

From the above observations, functional training will consist of exercises performed in an upright position, normally with feet in contact with the ground. They will add external stressors to the athlete to challenge stability and body control and will encompass whole body movements and sub-actions thereof. And they will naturally progress onto single leg variations that will be useful when performing in sports.

There are exceptions to the basic rules and when it is necessary we will address this. All exercises should have a purpose, and those that won't don't need to be in your programme and will not be in this book. That said, this is not an exhaustive text on what exercises are functional, but it will help to guide your decision-making as to whether it is useful to include the exercise that the excitable trainer at your gym may have recommended.

Functional training incorporates basic human movement patterns such as squatting, lunging and upper body pushing and pulling, in multiple planes of movement, and also bracing and rotating while in multiple positions. Functional athletes have the ability to control their own bodies; to master this ability is coveted highly by the functional training community and is desirable for continued injury resistance. An intelligent, functional athlete who is significantly better in one movement pattern will take action to balance the other patterns accordingly.

Keep in mind that functional training is the training of movement rather than specific muscle groups. Some hypertrophy may be functional but aesthetic hypertrophy tends not to be. Excessive strength in one area will typically lead to a less balanced movement profile, which may lead to injuries later on.

*Balanced movement profiles = better ability to meet external stressors in a sporting environment*

If having big bench scores is your thing, great! Try powerlifting; those guys show incredible feats of strength. Most people cannot even come close to competing with the numbers powerlifters rack up. On the flip side, how many powerlifters can perform multi-direction sprints for half an hour at a time?

*Unbalanced movement profile = unable to meet sporting stressors*

In anatomy lectures around the world, people have been taught the origins, insertions and actions an individual muscle creates when that muscle, in isolation is contracted. Many people are told daily a specific weakness exists within a specific muscle or generalized group, for example weak rotator cuff muscles, and that there is a need to train that specific muscle to provide injury resilience. They are told this by well-respected and educated professionals such as physical therapists who have performed isolation tests to identify which of the rotators are the culprits, with complete disregard of what is happening in the immedi-

ate vicinity and further afield to the muscle. It has been seen in many cases that those with rotator cuff injuries strengthen the tested and identified weak muscle yet do not gain the stability they are looking for within their sporting situation. This may be because the strengthening has allowed for a better test result to be achieved in a specific range of motion or against a specific type of force but is not necessarily of benefit to a fully functional sporting action that doesn't fall within the rotator cuff test procedure.

Physical therapists are extremely knowledgeable about some aspects of the body; however there are those who stick within the rigid framework of their teachings and fail to embrace the knowledge of other areas and professions. Some are extremely well-placed to work within athletic environments and hopefully more crossover of knowledge can occur to show different ways of achieving a goal and move away from the limitation tests that were conceived at the advent of modern physical therapy in the 1920s.

Educators in the strength and conditioning field have started to shift away from thinking in terms of single muscle actions and are now getting to grips with the kinetic chains of movement. A number of perspectives have been given on 'kinetic chains, slings or Anatomy trains'. They all relate to the concept that you need to look at the whole system rather than the isolated muscle to understand movement further. This understands that groups of joints and muscles work in unison to provide our movements, and that without a coordinated effort movement is always going to be lacking.

Muscles also do not act in only one type of contraction. They work across a spectrum of contraction types, and this is regulated by the need for the action to be accelerated, decelerated, mobilized or stabilized at a given point in time. Take a standard jump from a quarter squat as a starting point. The quadriceps, gluteals and calf musculature work concentrically to accelerate the athlete in a triple extension pattern of the hip, knee and ankle, respectively. This is not really different to what the traditional anatomy lecturers would tell you. However, when the inevitable occurs and the athlete descends to the ground because of gravity, the ankle, knee and hip will flex to absorb the forces.

However, what controls the movement and prevents the athlete collapsing into a heap? It is not the concentric contraction of the hamstring, hip flexors or tibialis anterior, it is the eccentric action of the muscles that caused the action, glutes, quads and calves. In addition, during the acceleration phase of the jump, the hamstring, hip flexors and tibialis anterior are not having a free ride. They are controlling the forces exerted by the quadriceps, gluteals and calf group by also working eccentrically, preventing the concentrically contracting muscles from producing too much force and causing injury to other structures through hyper-extension of the hips, knee or ankle.

By contracting in this way they provide stability, control and proprioceptive depth perception. Although a simple idea, by understanding that this is the case in most movements the body can make, we can start to understand that the musculature of the legs has a more important role than to contract and produce an agonistic movement and affects movement control further along the chain. By understanding this concept functional movement science becomes easily applicable in training a whole host of athletic disciplines.

By improving the function of the muscles when the athlete is in a standing position the muscular patterns and nervous stimulation become ingrained and the patterns improve; by isolating the muscles in machines the proprioceptive stimulus and the coordina-

tion of the multiple muscles involved in the action are lost. Thus the activity is not functional and therefore is not *purposeful*, so the benefits to performance are limited. They are limited because there will still be a performance stimulus; however the holistic approach of a functional programme gives you much more out for the effort you put in.

The aim of the programme outlined within this text is to create a strong, dynamic athlete that can perform in his or her sporting arena. In order to do that the programme must **build strength** where required that is specific enough to the sporting arena you are competing within but generalized enough to be useful in multiple scenarios. It must **build the connection** between the strength gained, the application of force and the movements we should be able to perform within the boundaries of human movement. These components are required in order to **build the performance** we are looking to achieve. At each step of building your individualized programme you should be able to identify which area you are looking to improve in order to affect your performance by the way in which the exercise is loaded, performed or the nature of the exercise (e.g. a mobility drill is designed to help your body achieve a better functioning range which maintains stability, therefore connecting the strength with the performance).

The book aims to arm you with the tools to identify your weaknesses, and address them, through building strength, functional hypertrophy, or corrective exercise using many different components including using both free weight- and body weight-orientated work, developing into sporting positions that will compromise the athlete's stability and cause a need for a reactive component of controlling the position, including single leg exercises. It is written to educate those who want to train in a way that has purpose to sport, whether new to the training game or having a little experience, but see so much conflicting advice. The advice produced here is the same advice athletes will receive throughout their training with me. There are no secret movements or protocols in functional training, just applying the ideas of what it means to produce functional movement within the training plans.

We always aim to move our athletes towards a level of strength and size that is useful to their sport but also to them as functioning humans. We aim to develop the ability to transfer this strength and produce powerful movements that when performed on the field of play allows athletes to perform to the best of their abilities. We use a slightly different approach to the traditionalists, but are not deviating just to be out there in our programming. It just makes sense to us to work in the way we do; it works for us and our athletes and can work for you.

CHAPTER 2

# HUMAN MOVEMENT

## The Human Structures

The body is made up of areas that are flexible and others that add stability. This is seen in the traditional teachings of the muscles with mover and stabilizer musculature. This idea is often missed within the joint structures of the body. There are some joints that are designed to provide a large range of movement and some to provide limited movement. Without the mobile joints such as the ball and sockets seen at the shoulder and hip, many human movements wouldn't be possible. Yet these structures need to be stable in their relationship to the body in order to perform in the way in which they are asked.

These areas of mobility and stability are alternating throughout the major areas of the body, as shown in Fig. 2.1.

As a general rule these sites alternate between the role of mobility and stability.

As you can see, the ankle starts as a **mobility** site. It is necessary for human function as an upright mammal. It allows us to move and adjust across uneven terrain, adds to extension activities such as walking and jumping, and provides a strong attachment for the lower limb musculature.

The ankle allows for around 50 degrees of plantar flexion, where the anterior angle of the foot is increased such as when tiptoeing; 15–20 degrees of dorsiflexion, where the

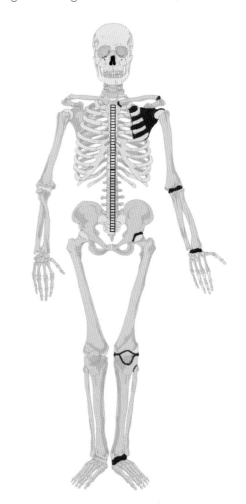

*Fig. 2.1  The human skeletal system. Areas in red are areas of mobility, while areas in blue provide stability, with less joint movement range. (Image: Wikimedia Commons)*

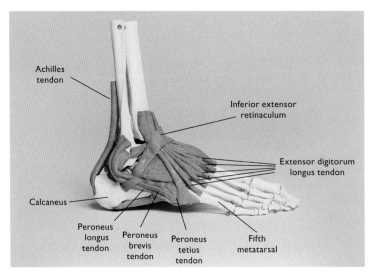

Fig. 2.2   *The ankle and foot.* (Photo: Nino Liverani/ Unsplash)

anterior angle of the foot is reduced; 20–30 degrees of inversion, where the ankle and foot is turned inwards so that weight bearing moves to the outside of the foot, such as in a common ankle sprain; and 5–15 degrees of eversion, where the weight is moved towards the inside edge of the foot.

This brief outline of the movements at the ankle highlight its ability to be a very mobile joint and thus an important one. Without its versatility it would not be as useful in its

role of balancing and righting the body. This joint comes under the mobility category of joints.

The knee is interwoven with connective tissues; ligaments, the patella tendon and associated structures, masses of musculature origins and insertion points. It is built and designed to work in primarily one plane: the sagittal. This provides a stable structure above the mobile ankle structure and can be a scapegoat for the hip and ankle if there are issues at those points.

Moving upwards into the hip joint, this is classified as a ball and socket joint. With appropriately balanced training this joint can provide a great deal of movement and be strong in those movements; however a lax joint without the strength to keep it in check will provide problems at some stage.

An overview of the possible range of motion at the hip demonstrates its versatility and primary role as a mobility zone; <130 degree hip flexion, <30 degree hip extension, <35 degree hip abduction, <30 degrees

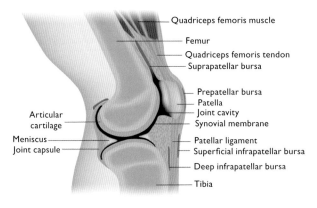

Fig. 2.3   *The knee.* (Image: Shutterstock)

of hip adduction and <45 and <50 degrees of internal and external rotation respectively. This highly mobile joint is categorized as a **mobility** joint despite its large bony architecture, strong ligament and the connection of the largest muscles in the body.

The next area of interest is the spine. The lumbar region is an area in which many people suffer with pain at some point in their lives. For some reason, many people sit and move from their lumbar spine, causing the lumbar region to be in a curved under position opposite to its standard position more often than it should. The L spine is one of the most frequently injured areas in sporting and non-sporting populations alike. Part of the issue is that people believe that their L spine can move more freely or be released by stretching past the extension and rotation that feels hindered. This is potentially dangerous, and I will show you why. What many do not realize is that this constant pressure on the lumbar spine overstretches the muscles that are trying to keep the spine straight and neutral. Allowing this curvature to occur places the cartilage discs under considerable pressure and often results in the disc 'slipping' or bulging, putting unwanted pressure on the spinal cord.

This is not the only negligence we show towards this structure. The spinal column also works within the three axes of movement. Slipping discs can occur in

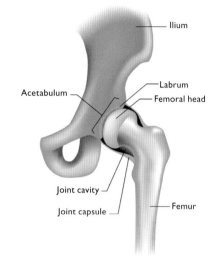

Fig. 2.4　The hip joint. (Image: Adobe Stock)

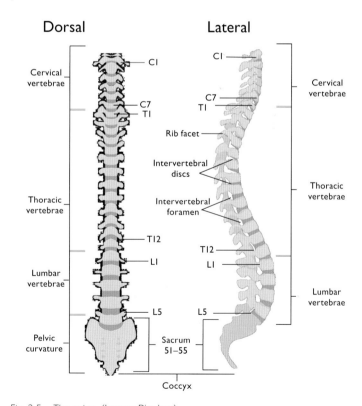

Fig. 2.5　The spine. (Image: Pixabay)

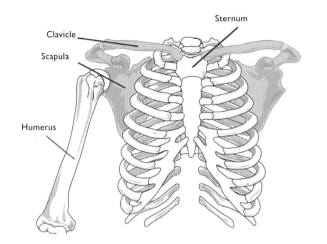

*Fig. 2.6   The shoulder girdle.* (Image: Wikimedia Commons)

excessive forwards OR backward rotation of a vertebrae; however the second common movement issue is rotating around the longitudinal axis. The individual vertebrae in the lumbar region are designed to make less than or equal to a 2 degree rotation away from neutral spine, either way. Compare this to its neighbouring region, the thoracic spine, which is considerably more mobile with up to 9 degrees of rotation available at each joint. These figures combined with the number of vertebrae give the total possible rotation available in each region as follows:

- Lumbar spine: five vertebrae, 2 degrees rotation at each, totalling 10 degrees of rotation available for the whole lumbar region.
- Thoracic spine: twelve vertebrae, each with 9 degrees of rotation, total rotation movement possible, 108 degrees.

The figures above highlight the greater **mobility** in the T spine over the lumbar region (12 × 9 = 108 degrees rotation vs 5 × 2 = 10 degrees). This also shows trainers and gym-goers how important it is not to over-rotate with the lumbar spine. It should be noted that rotating only 3 degrees per disc in the lumbar spine is enough to create micro-tears in the discs, and if performed regularly these micro tears can lead to greater issues that may

**Table 2.1   The language used in defining movement.**

| Language | Activity |
| --- | --- |
| • Knee-dominant activities – squatting<br>• Hip-dominant activities such as Romanian Deadlift (RDLs) – hip hinge<br>• (Horizontal) pushing and pulling<br>• Vertical pressing<br>• Torso rotation<br>• Braced core | • Squat<br>• Lunge<br>• Hip hinge<br>• Push-pull<br>• Rotate<br>• Brace<br>• May also include static stand and gait (run/walk) |

require surgical intervention. It is clear that the lumbar region is designed for **stability**, whilst the thoracic region has been built for **mobility**.

The next zone of interest is the scapula, which structurally is an irregular bone. Some bony structures are designed specifically for mechanical advantage; the kneecap is one and the scapula or shoulder blade is another. The scapula provides a large connective area onto which muscles attach. It has muscles whose purpose is to maintain its orientation and relationship with the ribs, thus providing stability; however, the mechanical advantage of the scapula comes when it is required to be in an elevated and rotated position to allow for the stability of movements involving the arms above shoulder height or orientation. Thus it is also a zone of mobility, depending on the needs of the movement.

The importance and complicated nature of the scapula's role is highlighted by the fact that it is unusual to have humeral movement (upper arm) without scapula involvement. During shoulder flexion, where the humerus is flexed above shoulder level, the scapula is in an elevated, abducted and upwardly rotated position. With gleno-humeral abduction above shoulder level the scapula is elevated with upward rotation. Adduction (retraction) of the humerus results in downward rotation, and a depression of the scapula; the same is included in humeral extension but also includes scapula adduction.

Horizontal adduction and internal rotation lead to the abduction of the scapula and also during external rotation and horizontal abduction. These roles will be important to consider when thinking about the basic human movement patterns and the preparation of movements.

With all this movement it would be easy to group the scapula into the mobility group; however the number of insertions of many muscles as mentioned previously shows it plays a role in the stability of this zone as well. This means it has a joint classification of **mobility/stability**.

As discussed above, the scapula works closely with the movements of the humerus. The humerus connects to the scapula at the glenoid fossa and completes the shoulder girdle with the clavicle. The junction for the humerus and scapular interaction is known as the gleno-humeral joint. This again is a ball and socket-type joint, which, as with the hip, is designed for a large range of movement (mobility joint). Again, with this large movement capacity there is a trade off with being prone to injury and impingements of tissues in and around the shoulder capsule. This joint is highly mobile due to the bone structures; it is also highly susceptible to injury due to the stability of the joint primarily coming from connective tissues.

## The Basic Human Movements

An increasing number of respected leaders in human movement have opened up the fitness world to the idea of basic human movements, a series of actions the body can and should be able to produce without limitations of age or gender. These actions in today's world can be lost as we are not the organisms we once were. Different authors and leaders in movement have labelled the movements in different ways but group the actions similarly.

## Differences in Approaches to Grouping Exercises

Different people describe the same action in different ways. Their experiences lead them to develop their own vocabulary to explain to their athletes in a way in which they are comfortable. By using different words and definitions, movements can fall under different categories depending on how the grouping word is used and is defined.

In some venues they may use squatting, lunging and hip hinging, in another, knee-dominant and hip-dominant patterns. Squats, lunges and hip hinges such as deadlift all fall under the knee- or hip-dominant labels but may mean the programme designed will look very different.

The basic differences between squatting and lunging are the stationary stance in squatting moves versus lunges involving a directional component. The squatting movement is quad-dominant, the lunges can vary as to which muscle receives the most stimuli according to the direction of the lunge. The hip hinge action requires the force to be produced by using the musculature around the hip to cause an extension of the hip from a hip-flexed position.

The difference between knee- and hip-dominant exercises can be seen by the angles of the main sections of the body, and Mike Robertson, a prominent practitioner in functional training in the USA, uses the following grouping method:

A **vertical torso** with an **angled tibia** defines a **quad- (knee-) dominant** pattern; this includes exercises within the squatting pattern.

Whereas an **angled torso** with a **vertical tibia** defines the **hip-dominant** pattern including the hip hinging patterns such as deadlifts and kettlebell swings.

Unfortunately this causes some confusion as to where a lunge should be placed, as a lunge has a **vertical torso** and a **vertical tibia**. This leads to a **lunge variation** grouping or the breaking of one of the rules to allow the lunge exercise to be included in either.

Hence you must choose one definition or the other; I group the exercise depending on whether the knee- or hip-dominant muscle group dictates the lunging movement. Lunges cross many boundaries and the purpose of that action will determine which group it is included in at any point in time. Thus, if we are looking to gain leg strength and load a lunge heavily, the quadriceps would be loaded and this would allow for the lunge to be placed under the knee-dominant group. However, we may use a split jump in which the torso is allowed to angle forwards to add in a stretch reflex of the posterior chain, yet the rearmost tibia is vertical and thus the application would allow this into the hip-dominant group.

## Push and Pulls

Some grouping of push and pull movements also have differences between them. Some include both the vertical and horizontal axes of both pushing and pulling, others will separate and not complete a vertical push and horizontal push in the same workout. Others deem it suitable to do so, the same with vertical pulls and horizontal pulls.

Within the functional training system we allow for inclusion of both vertical and horizontal axes because of the way in which we combine them within the phases of the programme to reduce the likelihood of overloading the pushing and pulling actions to the detriment of the athlete's abilities. More on this later.

## The Torso

A fully functioning torso requires it to be able to overcome a host of different challenges. It all starts with the ability to be strong within the neutral spine position.

The neutral spine is a position of strength that lies between a fully arched lumbar spine with an anteriorly rotated pelvis to a flattened arch and posteriorly rotated pelvis. By being in the middle there is always room for movement to buffer the forces should it be required, but also in this position the torso can produce and absorb forces in all three planes.

From the understanding of the neutral spine position we can then load the torso with problems to be repelled or overcome. Stuart McGill, the world famous 'back expert', stipulates that in order to train you should be able to achieve the following as minimum requirements.

- 2min full plank hold
- 2min back extension hold
- 90sec side planks, each side

Initially look to get the athletes to be able to endure 120sec (2min) of a plank, and when they reach this level, focus on the intensity over a shorter period of time and the ability to create force rapidly.

If you cannot achieve this level, we suggest you add in the plank circuit to each warm-up session, aiming to beat the last time by five seconds with perfect technique. Once you have achieved these levels and can meet them whenever required, as mentioned previously we look at working on the intensity of the holds. We reduce the time to multiple ten-second holds with emphasis on generating as strong a contraction as possible, adding an extra repetition of the squeeze up to ten repetitions before dropping back to four with longer durations and building up again. This works really well with our athletes and allows steady progress in the athlete's ability to produce a maximal contraction and more enduring efforts.

The next phase in building the torso is maintaining the neutral spine, creating a strong contraction and adding an upright posture to add a force coupling of the surrounding hip musculature. This means pairing up muscles diagonally opposite the joint, in this case the quads and the erector spinae couple to secure the hips and prevent posterior tilt while the hip flexors (psoas group) couple with the hamstrings to secure the hip and prevent anterior tilt.

Exercises to develop this phase include roll-outs, glute raises and tall kneeling cable lifts.

The next focus is looking at the development of the ability to neutralize forces exerted on the torso, particularly with regards to preventing rotation distractions within the lumbar region. This is where the torso work becomes much more functional in that the strength gained here translates into useable force during performance.

Exercises to develop this phase are more functional in that they alter the stability of the torso. They are the one-arm military press, one-arm cable press, Pallof press and variations and BB rotation (overcoming the rotation).

The final piece of the functional torso jigsaw comes in how we now apply the force through the torso in sporting performance. Many sporting actions require the rotation of the torso in order to perform the technique; tennis, golf, hockey, lacrosse, and combat sports such as boxing, ju-jitsu or wrestling all have actions requiring force production in a rotation action. This is where we look at introducing our power-based movements for rotation such as medicine ball wall slams or throws.

By looking at the torso we have produced a sequence that follows the progressions of the functional training system. Firstly, we look to build strength and make this strength connected to the performance of an action, before excelling this action into a power-orientated movement useful in a performance. The torso is the only area in which we aim constantly to develop or maintain the highest part of the continuum. We do revisit the lower level strength skills to ensure basic technical proficiency, but we would combine these skills with power moves to keep up the performance ability and reduce likelihood of injury.

## Bilateral or Unilateral, Two Sides or One – Which is Better?

Double leg exercises are characterized by solid foundations, large force production potential and even loading between each limb. They are great for increasing strength in specific movements; however they don't connect this strength with improved performance in the field of play. Single leg exercises allow for greater gluteus medius activity as well as increasing the contribution from the stabilizer muscles around the hip. However, some bilateral exercises are seen as better at replicating some sport-specific performances, such as a two-footed take-off when spiking a ball in volleyball or a jump shot in basketball. Bilateral exercises reduce the loading of each limb but also single leg variations tend to be unable to perform 50 per cent loading of the double

leg exercises. They also stress the proprioceptive mechanisms, which is a possible reasoning behind the less than 50 per cent loading figure.

## So Why the Need to Move into Single Leg Stance Exercises?

It has been shown that by increasing the stability within the hip, the force production in knee and hip dominant activities can be increased without structured training. This is because the bilateral stable activity (which is low on the functional continuum) has a larger proportion of contribution by the prime mover of the exercise. At the other end of the spectrum, the lower stability in the single leg work reduces the contribution of the prime mover in favour of the stabilizers. In an example of leg press versus the (Bulgarian) split squat with the rear foot raised, the prime mover in the leg press is the quadriceps, and very little stability is required as the athlete is seated. With the split squat, however, the athlete is in a narrow base of support, which kicks in the stabilizers, yet the load that can be lifted is significantly less. This load, however, may be closer to that which can be experienced in competition.

The split squat and lunge patterns also develop hip separation. This leads to an increase in the length of the hip flexors, which

---

**COACHING BOX**

- Try it for yourself. Stand up and change how your feet are in contact with the ground!

- Push your arches to collapse to the floor and see how the hips react. Now open up the arch.

in turn reduces the stretch experienced in the back. This often leads to an increase in the deadlift and squat loads achieved. Introducing hip separation to powerlifters is a tactic to better posture and shows the athlete that the excessive lumbar curve can be brought towards neutral and still gain strength, as we have found in athletes from powerlifting backgrounds and many other coaches will also have seen. It is not only those with powerlifting backgrounds that can benefit from this addition to their training. The knock-on effects of introducing the single leg work such as lunges and split squats is an increase in hip strength, as noted above. Having greater hip strength strongly correlates to having lower injury incidences in the lower limbs. Specifically, athletes complaining of shin splints or tendonitis of the lower limb will feel a reduction in their symptoms should they include hip separation exercises within their programmes. Some may even clear the injury completely.

To me it makes sense to include strength-building exercises from the bilateral group into our programmes to create stronger athletes. However it also makes more sense to increase the range of motion at the hip, increasing stability at the hip, because this leads to hip separation, which increases strength and power in functional movements and therefore on the playing field.

## Improving Single Leg Movements

The focus of working with single leg exercises is to improve stability at the foot, hip and pelvis. These three joints work together to perform fluid movement. Inability to function as they should leads to implications at one or more of the other sites.

Cause and effect changes to the foot and their impact.

Increasing foot pronation > tibial internal rotation > femoral internal rotation > anterior pelvic tilt

Increasing foot supination > tibial external rotation > femoral external rotation > posterior pelvic tilt

Some practitioners will focus on the fact that the foot has caused this occurrence of the effect on pelvic tilt. Some may not realize that what happens at one end of the relationship also affects the other in the opposite direction. Therefore having an anteriorly rotated pelvis caused by overactive erector spinae and overpowering quadriceps will equally be responsible for causing the femoral internal rotation, which will then lead to internal rotation of the tibia, too; now the foot pronates due to what has been happening at the top of the chain. The same is true for overpowering abdominals, and tightened or overpowered hamstrings causing the reverse effect and leading to foot supination.

Within the training, if you have either an anteriorly or posteriorly tilted pelvis you should aim to bring the tilt back to neutral and increase glute and oblique strength. This releases the hip flexors and the hamstrings, and allows the muscles to perform the actions for which they are designed.

Simple changes such as doing warm-ups barefooted and rolling a lacrosse ball for myofascial release in the foot during the warm-up can significantly alter the way you move and improve the imbalances within the lower limbs.

## Game-Changing Performance

The best athletes in the world differ from their peers because one or two components of their abilities are at a level that the peers' are not. If athlete A can squat their own bodyweight, then athlete B with the same physiology and anthropometrics who can squat more than their bodyweight is going to have an advantage in areas dependent on lower body strength, such as jumping. Some levels of strength or performance can be the difference between making the team and not making the team, scoring and not scoring, making the tackle or not. So it makes sense to aim for values that can provide game-changing opportunities for the athletes. That is what we try to get our athletes to strive for. If they hit all these targets then we are likely to have a champion in our midst; however having one of these game-changing scores is not enough, even two. You need to be able to perform across a spectrum of strength challenges in order to have a rounded athleticism, which will be game-changing.

Often young men, especially, will go to the gym and do the 'beach weights' to get the muscle definition in the key 'mirror muscles' and will forget the rest of their body. Often guys will put more time and effort into a bigger chest or biceps and forget about the lower body. But here's the secret. If you have the game-changing levels across the board, you'll get the body you desired, as a consequence.

What are these strength challenges and what do you need to achieve to have game-changer status?

Firstly, you need to be safe to train. So get on with the two-minute planks, two-minute back extension and ninety-second side planks.

Then you need to achieve good scores in the squat, bench, deadlift, pull-up and press-up categories. But we're getting ahead of ourselves here. We need to see where you are now and then how far the journey is to the game-changing status. So once you have the required pre-training abilities in the plank and back extensions you need to test your abilities in the five game-changer movements:

- Squat
- Deadlift
- Bench
- Maximum pull-ups
- Maximum press-ups

To get an idea of where you are depends a little on your training history. If you have lifted before for more than a year, then perform a simple reps test. Warm up with a bar and

**Table 2.2 shows the target ranges. The top value is the game-changing value in each category specific to age group.**

| Male | UI5 | UI8 | Adult | Female | UI5 | UI8 | Adult |
|---|---|---|---|---|---|---|---|
| **Back squat*** | 0.75–1.25 | 1.25–1.5 | 1.5–2.0 | | 0.5–0.75 | 0.75–1.0 | 1.0–1.5 |
| **Deadlift*** | 1.0+ | 1.5 | 2.0 | | | | |
| **Bench*** | 0.5–1.0 | 0.75–1.0 | 1.25–1.4 | | 0.5 | 0.75 | 1.0 |
| **Pull-ups** | 10+ | 15+ | 20+ | | 3-5 | 5+ | 10+ |
| **Press-ups** | 25+ | 35+ | 42+ | | 12 | 20 | 27 |

•Scores as a relationship to body weight.

complete five to ten repetitions with each load for two to three sets before reducing the reps to three to five while increasing the load each round. When you know you can't do heavier than the current load for three to five reps then finish and use the IRM calculator in the appendices to find your IRM. Plot these on the first testing grid.

If you haven't trained previously you want to perform ten reps each round until you cannot perform ten repetitions with good form. If form drops on the sixth repetition of a set, use that as a 6RM value for the calculator. Plot this on the first testing grid.

For the pull-ups and press-ups you want to perform as many as you can in a single effort. With the press-ups please note they should be performed at a pace of twenty-five press-ups per minute using a timing device.

The testing grid shows the target ranges for each test and the three male and female categories for the different ages. If you wish you can mark where these ranges are on the test grid and this will show you visually where you stand. Each score can be made into a percentage by dividing your score by the target and multiplying by 100. Take the average of the five scores to see where you stand in relation to game-changing performance.

This is your starting point; you may be closer in some areas than others or you may be way down the pecking order. Either way, this is now going to change as you have a plan to help you move towards these levels. We'll retest these after each training phase.

Work towards these scores across all tests and you will have increased you functionality and become closer to being a game-changer. Don't focus all your efforts on having the best bench, this will lead to having less function in another area. Build each area together and progress towards the goal on all fronts, not just one, or you'll end up being susceptible to injury.

CHAPTER 3

# FUNCTIONAL PROGRAMMING VARIABLES

People partake in training for numerous reasons. These are mainly for improving their appearance; i.e. losing excess body fat, increasing tone or muscle mass, or improving physical performance to become stronger, faster, 'fitter'.

Many believe the following equation to be true:

Gym work IN = Improvements in appearance/performance OUT

The exercises carried out during their gym sessions lead to the improvements they seek in the performance outside of the gym, i.e. within life or sports. What is often neglected is the amount of 'carry-over' from the work into the output.

For example, people going to the gym will go in and lift weights to get stronger. If they want to build a bigger chest they may use the chest press machine; if they are further down the functional continuum they may use dumb-bells. So often people will go and lift weights that are below stimulation levels for their outcome needs. Using 10kg dumb-bells for two sets of fifteen to twenty repetitions three times a week will not create the carry-over stimulation for an increase in chest musculature. Sure there may be a change in some shape as the tone of the muscle changes but very little, if any, hypertrophy will occur.

As another common example, many people will go to the gym to shift excess body fat and choose the cardiovascular (CV) equipment to do this. Why? How many fat Olympic marathon runners have you seen lately? Yes pounding the treadmill for hours will create a performance benefit; you will get more efficient at running. How does that benefit the mobile worker who runs for the train and has to carry his or her heavy luggage at the same time? The carry-over is lost as the external load is not replicated. Sure, they may not get out of breath so easily and may lose a little weight. The widespread running for fitness theory works on the basis that burning calories through running will allow for a negative caloric intake and therefore by not consuming as many calories and by exercising in this way their body will use the stored energy in the fatty tissue. The calories IN: calories OUT ratio is the simplest fitness concept. These people tend to know exactly how many calories are in each food, how long that chocolate bar will take to burn off, and will run for that duration in order to justify having it at lunchtime; 'It doesn't matter, I'll run it off later' is a common justification.

However, improving functional performance requires a little more thought than this. In order to design a functional programme to improve performance either in life or on the field, you must consider the components of functional training. For a truly functional programme you must consider each of these seven principal components:

1 Proprioceptive demand
2 Control of centre of gravity over the base of support
3 The correlation of the motor programme and relative timing within basic human movements
4 Open or closed chain exercises
5 Include all components of motor control system
6 Multi-planar movement
7 Integration of the components

# 1 Proprioceptive Demand

At muscular level, proprioception is governed by cellular sensors, known as neuromuscular spindles. These modified muscle cells are surrounded by a spindle-shaped sheath and have a varied nerve supply. The information relayed by these cells contains information pertaining to muscle length and tension. Similar receptors are found within other connective tissues, ligaments and tendons, to provide the CNS with the postural and positional information important to proprioceptive mechanisms.

Put simply, proprioception is the awareness of the body position in relation to the space it is within. Therefore, proprioceptive demand is how specific this information governing the body's relationship within a space is required to be.

To understand the demand you first need to understand the concept of a hierarchy of neurological command existing within the body and at what level proprioception is a component part.

## Levels of Neurological Control

There are three levels of neurological control – spinal, brain stem and higher centre/motor cortex levels. All pertain to different levels of information and feedback systems that are integral to human movement.

**Table 3.1   Levels of neurological control.**

| Spinal | – Involuntary |
| | – Completely unconscious activation |
| | – Primary spinal cord reflexes |
| | – Apply to smaller segments of the kinetic chain |
| **Brain Stem** | – Involuntary but actively aware |
| | – Primarily subconscious |
| | – Automatic synergies |
| | – Postural balance and righting reactions (proprioception) |
| **Motor Cortex** | – Voluntary |
| | – Conscious |
| | – Primarily preselected |
| | – Modified (compensated) primal patterns |
| | – Coordinated pattern of control |

Therefore, to reflect the neurological command hierarchy a functional exercise needs to take advantage of the following: use automatic spinal reflexes (expand, so that the reflex pathways are regularly used and are therefore in a state of readiness if required on the sports field); not suppress the automatic synergies or muscle pairings and kinetic linkages; challenge the body in a range of postural positions to challenge; balance and righting reactions (proprioception) at the brain stem level; and be integrated within the pre-learned primal movements to enable the facilitation of new and modified coordinated firing patterns at the voluntary, motor cortex level.

Returning to the issue of proprioceptive demand, the body is constantly receiving information via various stimuli from the surrounding environment and from within itself via feedback mechanisms. The central nervous system (CNS) governs and processes the information from the neurological command hierarchy to identify information pertaining to:

- Where the body is in relation to the world around (this includes where the limbs are in relation to each other and the centre of gravity (more on CoG later), and
- any movement the body is performing, in terms of the changes in the relationships of the component segments

The CNS employs a number of information gatherers via feedback mechanisms from the senses to perform its processing duties. These sensory receptors come in a variety of forms to provide various stimuli information, including visual (sight), auditory (sound), vestibular (balance) and mechanical proprioceptors.

The information processed leads to the commands the body receives to react to the stimuli.

Thus, if improving our function is to improve our movements in the world around us, it will require a large input from the CNS. A term used to provide an understanding of the relationship of the CNS within functional movement training is PNF, or proprioceptive neuromuscular facilitation.

Proprioceptive -> neuromuscular -> facilitation

This term literally means the environmental input (stimuli) leads to CNS (spinal level reaction) controls and kinetic chain (body part) interactions to produce motor responses of movement and muscle actions.

# 2 Control of Centre of Gravity over the Base of Support

Everything we do, every movement we perform in the gym, on the court, in the field of play, is affected by gravity. Unaided, we cannot escape gravity on earth.

**Positional Sense: Centre of Gravity, Centre of Mass and Base of Support**
Gravity's interaction with the body is not only in keeping it on the ground, but in affecting its relationship with the ground, i.e. balance. The control of balance is important in functional exercise because it is another factor that can be manipulated to increase the stimulus at brain stem level of the CNS, as discussed in the previous section. By controlling balance athletes can be better equipped to cope with the ever-changing environmental conditions around them, which can lead to injury prevention.

Many readers will have come across the term centre of gravity, the point at which the whole weight of an object can be considered to act. In regular-shaped objects it can be predicted, i.e. footballs, tennis balls and hockey balls. However, the human body is an irregular shape and invariably moves to complicate the CoG. Sometimes the CoG lies outside of the human body, such as in a pike dive in high board diving.

In balance, the mass of the athlete is also a factor. The centre of mass (CoM), the point in which the mass of the body is most concentrated, is also the point in which the sum of the moments of inertia (resistance to rotational forces) is zero; that is, this point is not affected by rotational forces.

To control balance, we need our bodies to be aware of the CoM in relation to its base of support (the region bounded by body parts in contact with a support surface or surfaces, such as the ground, that exerts a counterforce against the body's applied force. When in a single leg stance the base of support is the area within the outline of the foot). In order to correct the off balance situation the base needs to be changed to a level at which the momentum of the mass is negated or overcome.

For example, when standing upright, gravity will push down on us towards the centre of the earth. As we make our first step movement, gravity continues to draw us towards the centre of the earth; however the change from two feet to one and the movement of the CoM away from its base of support affects the equilibrium of balance. A rotational force acts upon the body with the trail foot, the foot in contact with the ground, acting as the fulcrum or pivot point, and gravity pulling the CoM towards the ground. Thus to prevent falling over, the lead foot must be placed beyond the CoM to counter the momentum and change the base of support into a wide supporting component. The faster the movement, the further in front of the CoM the foot is required to regain this equilibrium.

This principle relates to all exercises where a load, whether that load is a body part or external load, is moved away from the CoM, thus affecting the equilibrium of the body, i.e. in a reaching pattern. Adding an external load affects these interactions between the base of support and the CoM further by increasing the moments of inertia around that segment of the body. By using movements that affect the balance we can prime, stimulate and ready the brain stem level to be able to react to the balance challenges in not only sport or exercise environments but also daily life to prevent injuries through falling.

# 3 The Correlation of the Motor Programme and Relative Timing within Basic Human Movements

All repeatable skills have a motor programme. A motor programme is the sequenced signals stored within the central nervous system (CNS) that is sought after when the specific skill is required, and when initiated results in a specific sequence of coordinated movement. All sporting techniques are skilled movements applied to a situation, and they each have a set of signals, which in order will result in the desired skill being performed. During the learning phase, a skill may not have all the signals, or more likely not have the correct ordering of these signals in order to replicate the technique correctly or efficiently. Over time these actions will become ingrained, whether they are correct or not, and when called upon the action stored in the CNS will be replicated. This is why even basic movement patterns should be perfected tirelessly so that the motor programme, which has become autonomous, has the desired outcome without the potential for injury to the athlete.

When the skill or technique is being learned it is often the ordering or the sequence that is incorrect, or more often the speed of the sequence is not effective enough for the situation. Think about young children playing softball; they swing the bat but their reaction to the stimulus is lacking, thus the action of the swing is correct but hasn't got the relative timing of the sequence related to the situation. The ability to perform the motor programmes in correct sequence at the desired speed of autonomy is known as the relative timing. Add in a stimulus to which the motor programme needs to react and the skill becomes harder. If the timing is out, the action could mean the athlete misses a catch, misses the ball in a kick, or misses a block of a punch or kick. When timing is correct the movements look perfect, easy and effortless.

In terms of our basic human movements, we have learnt to walk, run, sprint, push, pull and rotate within our natural boundaries of movement. We produce these primal movements without need for correcting (exclude the intricacies of sprinting technique) and perform adequately in an autonomous way. These movements have the commonalties that they start and finish under complete control with correct sequencing of the concentric and eccentric phases required. When put into a sporting situation where we are needed to run, the biomechanical timing allows for the successful execution of the movements, time and time again, because the relative timing and the motor programme are an effective working partnership.

## 4 Open or Closed Chain Exercises

An open kinetic chain is described as the combination of several joints united successfully where the end or distal segment is free, such as during the leg swing phase during walking or running.

A closed kinetic chain is described as the combination of several joints united where the end or distal segment is in contact with the ground or apparatus such as in a pull-up, sweep rowing action or squatting in the gym.

In order for an exercise to be functional the exercise must replicate an action or skill that will be replicated. If the action Isolates part of an action, such as the leg extension exercise to improve running performance, the legs never encounter leg extension without coming into contact with the ground and thus the need to move from an open skill to a closed skill and allow the muscles to work as they would when the foot is in contact with the ground. More often than not, single joint exercises – exercises that have apparatus named after the prime mover or targeted area (e.g. chest press, leg curl and ab curl machines) – are typically open chain and are deemed less functional for athletic populations.

Exercises that incorporate multi-joint movement and involve the working limb coming into contact with the playing surface are likely to be in the closed-chain, functional category, but not always. Therefore it is necessary to expose the working muscles to movements that shift between open and closed chain activity in order to learn the suitable responses for as many activities as possible.

## 5 Include All Components of Motor Control System

Functional programmes should be aware of integrating many motor components, such as balance, flexibility, strength, power, agility, speed and coordination. That proves that the programming should be all encompassing, while allowing areas to be exclusive to certain goals at different times yet inclusive at others.

We see this statement as the ability to provide the athlete with the required motor component development appropriate to his or her rounded development. Therefore, if an athlete is overpowered in the quadriceps, we can be exclusive in developing hamstring strength as a remedy for this, while all other components in other movements are unaffected in the schedule.

Sometimes this means that athletes will be picked up on a potential injury cause and will have their programme altered in order to rectify the situation and prevent an injury from occurring. We may do this by increasing isolated strength, increasing the muscle size (functional hypertrophy), improving the range of motion about a joint or improving the ability to generate force quickly for stabilizing the joint.

By allowing for the focus to be altered in different movement levels we can continue to make functional gains in all areas specific to the needs of that area while addressing weaknesses or imbalances. This is a positive for the athletes involved as they are not excluded from training while they undergo rehab protocols with the medical team and continue to be part of the training group that maintains morale, focus and dedication. We find it also allows a quick return to play in most cases as there is less detraining effect than when athletes are excluded totally from a training group.

# 6 Multi-Planar Movement

We move in a variety of ways; our anatomy has evolved to allow us to perform our human functions. Evolutionary primal movement patterns as previously mentioned include pushing, pulling, running (lunge pattern), jumping (squat pattern) and twist (brace/rotational patterns). All of these primarily fit within a plane and an axis. Below outlines the cardinal planes and rotational axis.

## Cardinal Planes of Movement

**Sagittal plane** (anteroposterior plane). The sagittal plane is the splitting of the left and right halves of the body longitudinally. In this plane we can move forwards and backwards. The 100m sprint is performed primarily in the sagittal plane.

**Frontal plane.** The frontal plane splits the front (anterior) and back (posterior) halves of

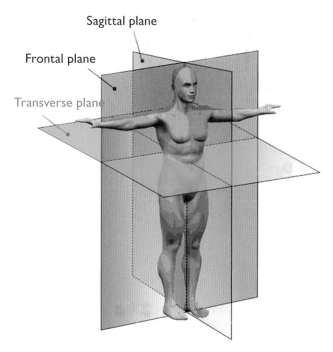

*Fig. 3.1   Planes and axes of the body.*
(Image: Wikimedia Commons)

the body from left to right. This is the plane in which lateral movements occur, such as the side shuffle.

**Transverse plane.** The transverse plane splits the body into upper (superior) and lower (inferior) halves, horizontally and at right angles to the longitudinal axis.

## Axis of Rotation

**Longitudinal axis.** An imaginary line running down the centre of the body, perpendicular to the transverse plane. Spinning movements such as those ice skaters and ballet dancers would perform (pirouette).

**Transverse axis** (medio-lateral). An axis that runs from side to side. Actions such as hip hinge or knee bend during a straight sprint would occur in this axis.

**Sagittal axis.** The axis that runs perpendicular to the frontal plane. A gymnast will perform a cartwheel around this axis.

The above descriptions of the planes and axes of movement all define in terms of isolated movements or rotations. However, movements are rarely performed solely in one plane or around one axis due to the number of segments of the body performing different movements at the same time and limbs altering their interactions with the body. As such, hybrid planes and axes are where most movements are performed. It is not the intention of this book to explain the many hybrids, however. So while I will relate exercises to a primary plane or axis, they may also have some relationship in another plane or axis.

For example, consider an overhead tennis serve. A player typically stands side-on to the service line and will rock away from and towards the direction of serve in the frontal plane and possibly be flexed at the hip (transverse axis) before lifting the ball up above their heads. They will jump within the sagittal plane and rotate around the longitudinal axis to transfer the power from the jump into the racket and into the ball. I hope this highlights the complexities of movements in a sporting situation and thus the need for multi-planar, multi-axial training for athletes to be prepared effectively for competition, whether that is weekend warrior or elite level athlete.

# 7 Integration of the Components

By bringing all of the components together we produce functional programmes. We know that to move along the continuum at some point there needs to be a change in the environmental pressures to challenge the proprioceptive demands; without this we cannot be sure the athlete can perform under a changing landscape and may be prone to injury. This is also vital in the constantly changing demands of both open and closed chain exercises to expose the athlete to conditions that replicate performance. Athletes must learn to control their bodies in relation to changes in the centre of mass relative to their base of support. They need to learn correct, efficient movement patterns to ingrain into the motor programmes they are required to perform in multiple planes of movement and in between, too. They have to strive constantly for balanced development in the motor components, such as strength, power, agility, etc, so that they are rounded athletes who are not overpowered in one area at the cost of weakened structures elsewhere.

By being selective in choosing exercises that develop and integrate the above components you can produce ever-adaptive yet structured sessions for you and others.

The system outlined in this book aims to cover all the integration of the components at various stages, often covering multiple components at any one time. The basic starting point is improving base strength in the key movements. Sometimes this requires a less functional approach or simply increasing the cross-sectional area of a muscle (hypertrophy) to produce greater strength qualities. The phases move into developing coordinated movements, which helps agility and balance, and produces revised motor patterns with better relative timing. They cover multiple planes of movement, with increasing proprioceptive demands being placed on the movements throughout the phases. Once through all the phases, the system then resets and starts once again to focus development on strength in the key movements, and we continue the steady all-round athletic development process.

## The Functional Paradox

With all the above being said regarding the integration of all components, there is an exception to this rule that lies within the stabilizer muscles in the body. These muscles play a completely different role in the function and protection of the human being; that is, they control the security and orientation of joints at all times. It is their job to fire most of the time to a level that keeps everything in alignment, and at crucial points where they are required to act as a shock absorber during trauma, or for example during a tackle in rugby, they are required to increase the firing rate to cope with this.

The stabilizers' ability to rapidly increase the rate of firing in the motor units can ultimately decide the outcome of a situation as to whether an athlete comes out unscathed or with an injury ranging from minor to serious depending on the point at which the stabilizers took control.

Therefore, it is important to understand that in order to improve the function of these muscles, they must be trained in a way that involves reacting to external stimuli from low-level stimulation to higher stimulation to recruit the necessary motor units.

In contact sports the head is required to be stable during contacts, and the muscles supporting this need are required to react and increase their activity in an extremely short period of time to prevent injury. The way to train an improvement in the rate of firing is to recreate the scenario in a more controlled situation.

This method can also be used to improve various chains within the body and is performed with a partner. The partner then takes the weight of the limb or head, the partner 'distracts' the athlete by gently moving the limb or head into various positions before quickly releasing the weight for the athlete to activate and control, or prevent the head/limb from dropping. This trains the rate of force development in the neck musculature and will aid the athlete in controlling forces applied to the head in contact and can potentially lead to a lower chance of concussion during a contact situation. This can be performed in both the sagittal and the frontal planes to create strength and knowledge of the technique before moving into movements between the planes.

This type of training should be performed under supervision of a professional who understands the mechanism.

Other stabilizers including the upper back stabilizers, the rhomboids, can be trained to be better stabilizers by simply waking them from their sedentary state caused by today's inactive lifestyles. For the rhomboids you

## YOUR FUNCTIONAL TOOLBOX

### Your own body

Your own body is the single most versatile, most complete part of anything within your own functional tool box. Many people forget how hard you can make an exercise by only using your bodyweight as the loading stimulus. For example, by moving your hand position within a push-up to an offset push-up you can make a push-up more difficult. What it also does is move the athlete along the functional continuum due to the new skills developed as a result of learning to press up from a less stable, more difficult situation than a regular press, therefore benefiting the human functionally.

### Weight Vests

Weight vests are great for progressing body weight exercise above the athlete's natural limit and create a greater stimulus for strength, growth and power. They can also be used within more advanced programmes to elicit a potentiation effect (more on this later) or in lifts where grip strength limits the ability to perform heavier lifts.

### Broom Sticks/Plastic Pipes

These modest pieces of kit can help in the assessment of imbalances, and traditionally that would be all they would be used for. However, they can be extremely useful training aids in terms of technical proficiency and coaching without fatiguing the athlete, but also can be used to strengthen extremely weak areas or improve movement patterns.

### Medicine Balls

A great piece of kit that normally can be thrown against a wall or floor, used for explosive passes and some core isolation exercises. They can also be of value when we are trying to disturb the athlete's equilibrium in proprioceptive training situations. But besides these uses it's useful to have an array of training aids in order to keep the athlete engaged with the ever-changing training sessions.

### Cable Towers

Cable towers are useful in providing directional resistance, which can be difficult to find in other equipment types. The pulley system allows for the effort to be made within the line of pull of the cable. They do have their limitations and have been replaced in more state-of-the-art gyms with hydraulic pulley systems (e.g. Keiser) which provide a constant resistance rather than a changing resistance as is found with a cable pulley system. However, functional strength gains can be elicited

can perform shoulder blade squeezes for a number of seconds to wake them up. Using this in your warm-ups and daily mobility exercises can dramatically improve your posture and subsequently your postural appearance becomes something to notice. Exercises such as the YTWs will help ingrain the purpose of the stabilizers in your upper back.

with either. If you have access to the hydraulic systems do use them; they are especially useful to those who have reached a plateau in their lifts.

## Barbell and Plates

A staple in most performance-orientated gyms, and creeping into the mainstream more so each year that passes. For real strength gains this external stimulus is one of the best, and it has a lot of versatility that some overlook within training programmes. Look out for better-quality bars, as there is a huge difference between the cheap mass production bars and the competitive standard ones. The most notable difference is in the maximum capacity rating or the maximum load that it is designed to take. Cheaper bars are not able to spring back from a huge deadlift and can become bent with no way of reversing the damage and straightening out the bar.

## Bands

Resistance bands have come to the forefront of fitness circles and then gone again a number of times. They have a number of uses, are light and can be useful for those who find themselves without a gym or who travel often. They can also be used to supplement gym work, whether body weight or free weight assistance work.

## Dumb-bells

Sometimes neglected in favour of the more fashionable barbell, the dumb-bell is an extremely useful piece of equipment that is great at exposing bilateral imbalances, and can be lifted, swung, pressed or pulled. Don't overlook this simple bit of kit, it could be the difference between the runners and the almost ran!

## Ladders

Ladders are great for speed and agility work, which if used with intensity can provide a variety of stimuli including high-intensity intervals, aerobic circuits, and the traditional speed and agility work associated with ladder drilling.

## Stability Balls

Seen in most studios and gym facilities around the globe, stability balls came to the forefront within antenatal groups and back pain management sessions. Although those are great uses, this piece of kit can take exercises to the next level of intensity, providing the unstable stimulus required to move the exercise along the functional continuum. However, they have been used in experimental exercises with adverse effects, mainly a bruised ego but also broken bones.

For knee stability it is recommended to work on the proprioceptive abilities of the lower limb. This allows real world stimulus for improving stability at the knee and is possibly one of the most important areas of training for sports that athletes forget. Adding proprioceptive work will reduce the likelihood of an ankle or knee injury occurring.

**Table 3.2    The functional continuum and examples of exercises.**

| Least functional ⟶ Most functional | | | | |
|---|---|---|---|---|
| **Lower body** | | | | |
| **Knee-dominant** | | | | |
| **Type of Exercise** | Leg press | Smith machine squat | Barbell squat | One-leg squat | One-leg squat on instability pad |
| **Rationale** | Sitting or lying, being held by the apparatus; no athlete-led stability | Standing with no stabilization from the athlete | Two legs, stability required | One leg, greater stability in the hip required | One leg on unstable surface; increased balance challenge at ankle |

| Least functional ⟶ Most functional | | | | |
|---|---|---|---|---|
| **Hip – dominant** | | | | |
| **Type of Exercise** | Leg curl | Back extension | Two-leg deadlift | One-leg deadlift/RDL | One-leg RDL on instability pad |
| **Rationale** | Prone, non-functional action | Prone, functional action | Standing | One leg, greater stability in the hip required | One leg on unstable surface, increased balance challenge at ankle |

| Least functional ⟶ Most functional | | | | |
|---|---|---|---|---|
| **Upper body** | | | | |
| **Horizontal press** | | | | |
| **Type of Exercise** | Machine-based bench press | Bench press | Dumb-bell bench press | Push-up | Stability ball press-up |
| **Rationale** | Supine, no athlete stability required | Supine, moderate stabilization | Supine, individual arm stabilization | Prone closed chain | Prone, with balance challenge |

| Least functional | | → | Most functional | |
|---|---|---|---|---|
| Vertical press | | | | |
| **Type of Exercise** | Lat pull-down | | | | Pull-up/chin-up |
| **Rationale** | | | | | |

| Least functional | | → | Most functional | |
|---|---|---|---|---|
| Horizontal pull | | | | |
| **Type of Exercise** | Machine row | Dumb-bell row | Inverted row | One-arm, one-leg row | One-arm, two-leg row with rotation |
| **Rationale** | | | | | |

| Least functional | | → | Most functional | |
|---|---|---|---|---|
| Torso exercises | | | | |
| **Type of Exercise** | Crunch | Russian twist | Standing lift | Standing lift with rope | Medicine ball rotation throws |
| **Rationale** | Lying, no rotation | Lying, with rotation | Standing no movement | Standing weighted movement | Standing explosive movement |

# CHAPTER 4

# KNOWING YOUR TYPE

Without doubt, some workout progressions just work; no questions asked, they just do. They tend to be very simple and very effective at doing what they say they will do. An example of this is the 5 × 5 method and its variations. Essentially all that is asked of the athlete is to perform the squat, bench and bench pull/bent row for five sets of five repetitions. If completed with perfect form, add some more weight the next time you train.

A ton of athletes have used this or a variation of this programme to get stronger fairly quickly. However, some have less than expected results due to not understanding how much load will trigger the responses they ask. As mentioned in section one, using too low a load for more repetitions will not really pack on any mass or strength, neither will low weight, low reps. When a rep scheme is given the maximum load you can perform for that exercise across all sets is when the last one of each set is close to failure. So the fifth of each set should be difficult in the above programme.

The programme outlined within this book is a variation of a number of programmes I have run that have allowed steady progress for many of the athletes I have worked with. Over time these have been modified and tweaked to maximize the individual athlete's goal. Now they come together in what is arguably the best system of training principles I have put together in one programme. This has drawn on many successes and failings that have unfolded over time, and taken in snippets of information, concepts and innovation from all the training systems I have used personally and for my athlete groups.

Over this coming section I will show you how I go about building a programme that fits into everyone's time availability to train. It is partially down to prioritizing your time towards the bang for your buck exercises, which can be influenced by your body type.

## Body Types

Your body type is the way in which your body is made up, and there are three main somatotypes. You will fall within the web of these three, although not necessarily exclusively in one type.

- **Mesomorphs** are those horrendously genetically gifted guys and girls who simply look at the weights in front of them and achieve their desired outcome. Typically they will look more muscular and have lower body fat without much need for training. Think the typical well-built, outgoing 'Jock'-type guy from American high school movies typically associated with power-based sports: rugby, American football and Olympic lifting. The genetic gifts they have been given include low body fat due to lower carbohydrate sensitivity and fantastic insulin regulation in their early years into adulthood. They put on muscle easily as a result of wide bone structure, which is beneficial when building muscle to enhance performance.

- **Ectomorphs** are the tall skinny ones. They have fantastic levers, typically can eat a horse and have burned it off before they have finished getting up from the dinner table. Again, they have low levels of body fat, but also have difficulty in putting weight on. These athletes will typically be geared towards endurance sports or sports where height is an advantage.
- **Endomorphs** are the unfortunate ones. They can be strong but hold weight, especially excess body fat, extremely well and are able to put on more very quickly. Losing weight is often difficult for this body type. A slow metabolism is repeatedly used as an excuse for this body composition.

How to find out where you fall within the radar chart of somatotypes is often difficult for an average gym user. Typically, people will be identified by their appearance:

- Tall and skinny, narrow hips and shoulders, rectangular shaped – ectomorphs
- V-shaped torso – mesomorphs
- Square shaped, fat carrying – endomorphs

These assumptions are often wrong in terms of the genetic blueprint of a person. A functional programme will look to enhance and optimize the athlete's genetic features and create an adequate amount of muscle mass. In order to do this identifying the potential of your frame and closer identifying the somatotype will aid with the selection of appropriate sets and reps schemes.

A way of aiding your knowledge of your somatotype is to identify a few measurements and the relationship of the measurements to each other, as outlined by nutritionist Dr John Berradi. I have simplified the scoring so you can identify which somatotype you fall into from these measurements.

You will need to note down the measurements in Table 4.1. Fill in the chart or use a separate sheet to make your calculations.

**Table 4.1   Body composition measurements.**

| | | Measurement (cm) |
|---|---|---|
| **Height** | A | |
| **Torso length:** Measure the distance between the acromion process at the top and front of the shoulder and the top of the iliac crest of the hip | B | |
| **Femur length:** Measure the distance between the greater trochanter on the outside of the top of the femur and the lateral condyle of the knee | C | |
| **Tibial length:** Measure the medial condyle (inside of the knee) to the medial malleolus of the ankle | D | |
| **Bi-acromial breadth:** Distance between both acromion processes of the shoulders | E | |
| **Bi-Iliac breadth:** Distance between the iliac crests of the hips | F | |

**Table 4.2   Somatotype scoring grid.**

| Somatotyping Relationships | | | |
|---|---|---|---|
| 1   Shoulder to hip ratio | Divide E by F | |
| 2   Femur–torso length relationship | Divide B by C | |
| 3   Tibial length versus torso and femur | Divide D by B | |
| | Divide D by C | |
| 4   Shoulder width–height relationship | Divide E by A | |

## What Do the Relationships Indicate?

The endo–meso–morph scale (see Table 4.5) shows the excess fat-carrying and/or muscle-building ability of your frame. Mark the point on the scale to show where you fall.

**Relationship 1:** Identifies the likelihood to carry muscle mass on the frame. A figure of around 1.46 is optimal for adding muscle mass. A figure of equal to or less than 1.00 identifies a likelihood of endomorphy, or ability to carry fat easily.

Mark point 1 for value of <1.00

Mark point 2 for a value between 1.01–1.15

Mark point 3 for a value between 1.16–1.25

Mark point 4 for a value between 1.26–1.40

5 points if a value >1.41

**Relationship 2:** Identifies whether you will have difficulties in some of the lower body big lifts, i.e. squat and deadlift. If your femur is significantly longer than your torso you will need to lean further forwards in order to reach the depth required. This is an expression of ectomorphy. No points awarded, although you need to be aware of some of the difficulties you may encounter in the ' Big Three' lifts.

**Relationship 3:** A shorter lower leg with an equal torso and femur length will pose similar problems to the above, if you have a shorter lower leg than both the femur and the torso you will require additional range of motion at the ankle to manage the ability to reach depth adequately.

Determine your ectomorphy by points:

1 point for a torso which is <95% of the femoral length

1 point for tibial length <95% of femoral length

1 point for tibial length <95% of torso length

0 = less ectomorphic, 3 = very ectomorphic

**Table 4.3   A comparison of height and shoulder widths.**

|  | Height | Shoulder width | Difference height–shoulder width | Width/Height |
|---|---|---|---|---|
| A | 1.85 | 0.35 | 1.50 | 0.189 |
| B | 1.85 | 0.38 | 1.47 | 0.205 |
| C | 1.75 | 0.35 | 1.40 | 0.200 |
| D | 1.75 | 0.38 | 1.37 | 0.217 |

**Relationship 4:** The difference between the shoulder width and the athlete's height determines the ectomorphy of the person. A taller person with the same shoulder width will exhibit greater ectomorphy than their shorter counterpart; as such the figure will be lower.

This figure shows that the discrepancy between the height and the shoulder width is more of a factor in ectomorphy than each individually. A lower score than 0.200 would suggest greater ectomorphy. If you score this, add a point to the ectomorphy scale.

Now plot this on the grid in Table 4.5 to estimate where you lie on the somatotyping scale.

The somatotyping you have will dictate the sets and reps patterns you will respond to best for hypertrophy. When it comes to writing your sets and reps into your programmes you can use the values given in the following chapter for the hypertrophy portion of the programmes.

**Table 4.4   Ecto/endo–meso scores.**

| ECTO Score (0-4) | ENDO-MESO Score (1-5) |
|---|---|
|  |  |

COACHING BOX

Additional ankle mobility work is often necessary in those with long fibula scores. If this relates to you, pay attention to completing mobility drills within the programme even more.

**Table 4.5    Somatotype grid.**

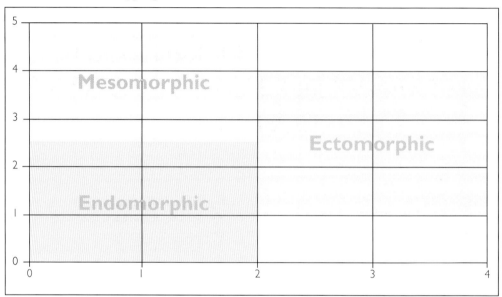

CHAPTER 5

# PROGRAMMING CONSIDERATIONS: STRENGTH, SIZE AND POWER SCHEMES

Within training, the common terminology regarding how much, how many and how often we perform exercises is contained within common nomenclature. Repetitions, or reps, are the individual actions of performing the exercise from start position to finish position once. In a bench press this would be from the arms locked out position, bar lowered to the chest and returned to the start position. This would be a single repetition.

Reps are often performed multiple times together. Once the required number of repetitions has been lifted this would be known as a set of repetitions, or simply a set. Multiple sets are common in programmes across the world.

It must be understood that there is an inverse relationship between reps and sets. If high repetitions are used, then sets should be kept to a minimum in order to ensure correct technique and prevent patterning of poor technique when fatigued. At the opposite end, low reps may be completed in a higher number of sets. The inverse relationship helps to prevent neural overdrive. The nervous system can withstand a certain amount of bombardment, but past that it fails to work correctly. So understand that if you are doing higher reps for strength endurance you shouldn't be completing as many sets as when in strength and power load ranges.

Load is the amount of weight within the external resistance, whether that is a barbell, kettlebell or medicine ball. When completing exercises you will often base the load on a percentage of the maximum you can lift for one, three or five reps during a test. Within the programmes contained in this book, you will find out what your starting point is and then add load as you get stronger.

When working to reps and sets in your programmes, the reps outlined in the reps column in Table 5.1 are designed to be indicative of being a struggle for the last one or two reps of each set. This is the way we bring about the neurological and physiological adaptations required to get bigger, faster, stronger and more functional. The table shows the max reps and suggested maximum number of sets at those loads. As you can see, the table shows the inverse relationship explained above.

Traditionally the loads assigned to maximum repetitions have been fairly strict in their zones for their required outcome: power in the low reps, very high load (as a percentage of IRM); strength in the low-mid-range reps and high load.

**Table 5.1   Reps max vs sets max.**

| Reps (Max.) | Sets (Max.) |
|:---:|:---:|
| 2–5 | 5–7 |
| 12–15 | 2–3 |

However, not everyone is built the same. And so there are different strokes for different folks, as they say. I hope to shed some light on this in this next section as to what is required for the ectomorph, mesomorph and endomorph in terms of loads for various goal responses to training ranges.

Within the programmes that we create, we input pieces of the puzzle from various protocols we have implemented successfully within our training programmes. It is these tried and tested methods that have been influenced by years of research and trials in our own training plans, research, and team training sessions. The component parts have all been used, tweaked and developed further through our experiences. These components work so long as they are followed and performed intensely!

The following section outlines some of the components that will be incorporated into different areas of the programmes you will create later on.

**Table 5.2   The reps continuum.**

| %1RM | 100 | 97 | 93 | 90 | 87 | 85 | 80 | 75 | 70 | 65 | 60 | 55 | 50 | 45 | 40 | 35 | 30 | 25 | 20 | 15 | 10 |
|---|---|---|---|---|---|---|---|---|---|---|---|---|---|---|---|---|---|---|---|---|---|
| RM | 1 | 2 | 3 | 4 | 5 | 6 | 8 | 10 | 12 | | | | | | | | | | | | |
| Traditional Target Ranges | | Power | | | Strength | | | Hypertrophy | | | Endurance | | | | | | | | | | |
| Endomorph | | | Power | | | Strength | | | Hypertrophy | | | | | | | | | | | | |
| Mesomorph | | Power | | | Strength | | | Hypertrophy | | | | | | | | | | | | | |
| Ectomorph | | Power | | Strength | | | | | | | | | | | | | | | | | |
| | | | | Hypertrophy | | | | | | | | | | | | | | | | | |

# The 345 Scheme

The 345 scheme takes the stand that we can overload the body to create a stronger and more enduring body at a given load (~85% IRM) fairly consistently in athletes new to structured programmes. By increasing the volume through increased number of sets the load can remain at a high percentage of our maximum and still increase our strength and the endurance of those muscles to perform that movement or exercise. Traditionally this scheme has been used with a 5RM. In untrained athletes or those new to weight training, this is a good starting point. The 5RM will increase your strength levels in the lifts consistently for a good period of training before the chance of any plateaus occurring. However, this method can also be used in hypertrophy work and for power endurance with great results.

The beauty of the 345 scheme is that it is easy to follow. Complete the required number of reps for the required number of sets twice and you have earned the right to add a set up to five sets. If you have a bad day lifting between completing the required sets then it is up to you to be honest with yourself and say whether you truly can complete the sets with correct form and increase the sets or, if sets are maxed out, to drop the sets and increase the weight on the bar.

# Fx Strength 345 Scheme

From the rep ranges schema, you will see that for strength all body types react to a stimulus that is equivalent to a 5RM load. The 345 scheme exploits this commonality within lifters.

This set scheme is where the reps remain the same, but the sets increase from 3 to 4

to 5 over subsequent sessions in which the load lifted was lifted with correct technique; each level, i.e. 3, 4 and 5, will take a number of sessions to get to the point where all lifts are made with correct form, at that load. During the final set, it is more important to maintain form than achieve the number of reps. If not all reps are achieved, aim for one more in the final set the next time you complete that exercise, and so on until the set is completed. When you have achieved the full number of reps and sets for two sessions you may add another set. Once five sets have been completed you increase the load by one plate (1.25 or 2.5kg either side) and drop down to three sets with the increased load.

For example:

**Session 1:** Target 3 × 5 @ 50kg: completed all bar last rep

**Session 2:** Target 3 × 5 @ 50kg: completed all with technique

**Session 3:** Target 3 × 5 @ 50kg: completed all with technique

>**Completed schemes of 3 × 5 twice**

**Session 4:** New target 4 × 5 @ 50kg: completed 3 full sets + 3 reps of last set

**Session 5:** Target 4 × 5 @ 50kg: completed 3 full sets + 3 reps of last set

**Session 6:** Target 4 × 5 @ 50kg: completed 3 full sets + 4 reps of last set

**Session 7:** Target 4 × 5 @ 50kg: completed 3 full sets + 4 reps of last set

**Session 8:** Target 4 × 5 @ 50kg: completed 4 full sets

**Session 9:** Target 4 × 5 @ 50kg: completed 4 full sets

>**Completed schemes of 4 × 5 twice**

**Session 10:** New target 5 × 5 @ 50kg: completed 4 sets + 2 reps

**Session 11:** Target 5 x 5 @50kg: completed 4 sets + 3 reps

**Session 12:** Target 5 x 5 @50kg: completed 4 sets + 4 reps

**Session 13:** Target 5 × 5 @50kg: completed 4 sets + 4 reps
**Session 14:** Target 5 × 5 @ 50kg: completed 5 sets
**Session 15:** Target 5 × 5 @ 50kg: completed 5 sets
  **>Completed scheme of 5 × 5 twice**
**Session 16:** New Target 3 × 5 @ 55kg

With this scheme, for some of the big lifts you can continue to build strength and volume gradually over many weeks without a specified de-load week as seen in some programmes. A de-load is necessary when the volume becomes too much too consistently for the nervous system to take. As you can see from the graph in Fig. 5.1, once the steps have been taken to get up to 5 × 5 the volume drops dramatically (450kg of loading) when you up the load to 55kg from 50kg and return to the 3 × 5 scheme.

This concept was first brought to me through the work of Mark Rippetoe. It is highly effective in beginners to the squat, deadlift and bench. We use a variation of this method in the foundations programme for the Big Three exercises.

## Hypertrophy Schemes

We have discussed a number of differences in the lift techniques for different body types and noted some variations in building strength. Variations in how to build size also occur with different shapes responding to slightly different hypertrophy stimuli. We have defined these to be easily identifiable for each somatotype. Typically those in each of these body types will react favourably to the schemes outlined below.

Both the meso- and ectotrophic schemes follow the same principles. The first set awakens the muscle group into working, the second excites the higher threshold fibres therefore increasing the number of fibres working

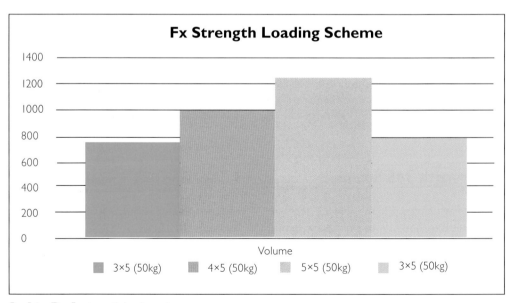

Fig. 5.1  The Fx strength loading scheme.

during the exercise, and the third set fatigues the fibres and provides the crucial damage required for hypertrophy adaptations. By using this method you can develop strength across a spectrum on the strength power curve and produce a hypertrophy adaptation. Effectively, this hybrid can be used to produce increases in strength, also however our primary use is to build hypertrophy in as many fibres as possible by including the higher threshold fibres.

Loads for each set:
Mesotrophy Scheme: Set 1: 8RM
Set 2: 5RM Set 3: 10RM
Ectotrophy Scheme: Set 1: 6RM
Set 2: 4RM Set 3: 8RM

The added benefit of this scheme is that each set can develop independently of each other. For example, the first time an athlete attempts the scheme he or she may complete the eight reps in the first set, four in the second but feel they had more left in the last set. The next time the first set load is maybe increased by 2.5kg, the second set remains the same, and the third also has 2.5kg added. The next time the athlete comes across this workout again they may get seven out on the first set, five on the second and ten on the third. The third time they can add extra load to the second or the third set. Once the athlete is around the correct loads for each set it is advised to only add weight in one of the sets in the next session.

Some athletes will progress in the third set but not in the first, thus the load in the third set can be the equivalent of the repetition max of the first set, yet they can push out an additional two repetitions therefore altering the RM. This phenomenon is a result of post-activation potentiation (PAP), this is what is trying to be induced by the second set load. When this occurs the next increase should be

**Table 5.3    Fx Mesotrophic – Eight-Five-Ten Scheme.**

| Set 1 | Set 2 | Set 3 |
|---|---|---|
| 8 | 5 | 10 |
| 8RM or ~80% 1RM | 5RM or ~87% 1RM | 10RM or 75% 1RM |
| 65kg* | 70kg* | 60kg |

*nearest plate total to percentages vs 80kg 1RM

**Table 5.4    Fx Endotrophic Six-Four-Eight Scheme.**

| Set 1 | Set 2 | Set 3 |
|---|---|---|
| 6 | 4 | 8 |
| 6RM or 83–85% 1RM | 4RM or ~90% 1R | 8RM or 80% 1RM |
| 67.5kg* | 72.5kg* | 65kg* |

*nearest plate total to percentages vs 80kg 1RM

**Table 5.5   Fx Ectotrophic Ten-Twelve-Fourteen Scheme.**

| Week | Session | Load* | Sets  Reps Fully completed |
|:----:|:-------:|:-----:|:--------------------------:|
| 1 | 1 | N | 3 × **10** |
| 2 | 2 | N | 3 × **12** |
| 3 | 3 | N | 3 × **14** |
| 4 | 1 | n + 2.5kg | 3 × **10** |
| 5 | 2 | n + 2.5kg | 3 × **12** |
| 6 | 3 | n + 2.5kg | 3 × **14** |
| 7 | 1 | n + 5kg | 3 × **10** |

*Load equals 75% 1RM at the start of this programme. After this, base the loads on what you started with plus a plate as you complete the 3 × 14 and ignore percentages thereafter.

added to the first set to restore the balance in the programme. This is shown in an example below.

The endotrophic scheme is based on adding an element of fat loss to the programme. As endomorphs are carrying a little extra, they typically need a metabolism boost. Thus the higher repetition range causes this. In addition to the metabolic advantage, endomorphs will naturally produce IGF-1, or Insulin-like Growth Hormone 1, which aids in the production of an anabolic state required for hypertrophy. This scheme involves three sets of the same load. However, like the Strength 345 scheme, the volume increases, in this case each week for three weeks by adding two repetitions to each set. This keeps the workout time for this exercise level fairly constant as it may add ten to fifteen seconds per set rather than three to five minutes each time the volume increases as in the 345 Scheme, which is necessary due to the extra rest time when adding an additional set.

# Training for Power Development

Within the power training phase we are looking to get the muscles as highly recruited as possible across all types of muscle fibre. In brief, the muscles have two types. Type I are slow twitch; these are your endurance fibres, have large volumes of myoglobin and mitochondria, and produce slow, low-level contractions by producing large amounts of aerobic energy through the aerobic production of ATP. They are more often found in stabilizing muscles in the neck and spinal structures because of the enduring capabilities. Distance runners will naturally have higher Type I fibres although this is not only a genetic expression but is enhanced through training.

The Type II fibres in basic level physiology have two sub-types: IIa and IIb. Type IIa (also known as fast oxidative fibres) are the in-between Type I and Type IIb fibres. They produce stronger contractions, are able to generate energy through both aerobic and anaerobic means and have large numbers of mitochondria and myoglobin, but not as many as Type I, and thus are more prone to fatigue.

Type IIb (also known as fast glycolytic fibres) are great at breaking down ATP stores very quickly. However, due to their low myoglobin and mitochondria levels are not great at producing it, therefore they run out very quickly. These fibres are great at producing rapid, explosive contractions over less than ten seconds' duration.

This information is important in understanding the next concept, the speed-strength curve. This is the relationship between the speed of the muscle action against the amount of strength forces produced. In maximal strength exercise, the speed of the action is slow but the strength required to move the resistance will be high (note that the intention may be to go as quick as possible but the action is still slow). Think maximum single squat (100% or IRM). At the other end of the curve we have maximum speed. These are against low resistance (<30% IRM) but at maximal speed. Think of a vertical jump test.

Between these extremes are the trainable components. These are strength-speed, which works on forces applied to intensities of 75–90% IRM, power (40–60% IRM range) and speed-strength 30–60% IRM. We perform the strength-speed exercise first to ensure quality movements that are explosive in nature but recruit large numbers of Type IIa fibres. We then recruit the higher threshold.

Using this information we can get the muscle to be capable of performing better in each of these ranges following training. Developing max strength will mean that the previous maximum will be moved quicker and most likely increase the number of times it is rep'd for. The new maximum is higher, therefore all percentages of this are higher

and the curve looks to have shifted right while extending. Building strength will allow more repetitions at lower intensities and is a key reason for performing maximum strength training. However, when we want to optimize performances across the whole range we need the muscles to become used to working at that level of resistance.

With the idea of use it or lose firmly within training philosophy, i.e. if you stop lifting heavy you lose that ability to do it, we have found a protocol that allows us to hit the main points on the curve, to increase the competitive power output range of an athlete without losing maximum strength ability. This has been termed French contrast training online but hasn't, as far as we are aware, been paired closely with the force velocity curve as our use of it does.

We start with a heavy compound lift (75–90% IRM) and follow this with a maximum strength lift (>90% IRM). We then perform a body weight or light-loaded speed exercise (<30% IRM) followed by the performance optimizing power or speed-strength (30–60% IRM) exercise. This order is designed to aid the final explosive exercise by having recruited the most fibres possible and getting them to perform in lower-level activities.

We use the strength-speed load for multiple, quality technical lifts. This is at the maximum strength level to recruit the highest threshold fibres, because once primed these are easier to recruit again. We encourage faster lifting speeds through the max speed exercise. All these stimuli, higher threshold fibres, speed of movement and moving heavy things quickly, contribute to higher force output in our mid-ranged, optimally loaded exercise. By repeatedly training the muscles to recruit the high threshold fibres and perform in low-threshold actions we hope to ingrain the recruitment of these higher-threshold fibres when in compe-

**Table 5.6    French contrast training loads.**

| | |
|---|---|
| Compound exercise strength-speed exercise | 6 repetitions of a 10RM load |
| Compound exercise max strength | 2–3 repetitions of 4RM |
| Max speed | 8–10 repetitions of light load (<30% 1RM) |
| Max power output | 5–10 repetitions of 30–60% 1RM* |

*exercise optimal load for Peak Power Output (PPO) dictates the load, see Appendices.

tition and therefore have a more powerful athletic action. Also, because of covering all aspects of the force velocity curve, we maintain maximum strength levels at the same time as we develop the ability to express the strength we possess at levels of resistance in athletic performance.

For the upper body we use a contrast of heavy and light in a super set or contrast training for the push and pull variants. Alternating between a superset of each of the upper horizontal push and vertical pull in one workout, and vertical push and horizontal pull in the other.

# CHAPTER 6

# EXERCISE PROGRAMMES

Within the training community, each specialty has something to offer another. Protocols, exercises, rationale, coaching process – everything has a place. It is hard to deny that some programmes just work: some lifts are greater in the training response, cross over into sporting situations, or are better at preventing or rectifying a movement deficiency.

With this in mind, the following section is about selecting exercises and gives progressions, regressions and time efficiency selections for you to build your programme. The purpose of this is to allow you to train intelligently, effectively, and with purpose every time!

## Differences between Traditional Linear Programmes and this Functional Training Method

### Exercise Rotations to Build, Connect and then Perform

Many programmes will follow linear periodization and you will only perform strength exercises within the strength phase and power in the power phase. These work fine, and in some cases are brilliantly executed. However, we have found with most sports having long in-seasons we can elicit specific changes that will accelerate the athlete towards the optimal by working a linear periodized plan for each level of movement separate from each other. The idea of this programme is to work on the areas that will individualize the needs of you or the athlete while creating functionality, rather than just using one training phase for each component of fitness.

The programmes we provide combine building towards and connecting to performing optimally in the sport or challenge. Each movement will more than likely not follow the same chronological programming from pure strength moves to pure power performance moves. You may need to build more strength within the squat pattern, and be able to connect the strength you have in the upper push with your performance. As such, at different times you may be within different parts of the continuum and therefore the focus required for the squat will lead you into choosing the foundations template. This will allow for the squat to be placed in the building section and the upper body in the connection section.

If you identified that you are not in control of the strength you possess, surely it makes sense to gain that control before adding more strength that cannot be controlled, and therefore will not be useful within your performances. This may be a different approach to many programmes; however we feel it provides flexibility within the programme to advance in strength, size, coordination and power at the same time across the whole body and this doesn't hamper the gains of one area in order to produce gains in another.

A number of linear models have been developed, using different labels for different periods. Matveyev's six phases is one such linear periodization model, where the phases are based on six periods. The first two periods concern general preparation work, generalized body conditioning, and include some areas to be developed throughout the year. The third and fourth periods involve competition-specific training and may include minor competitions to gauge the competition readiness of the athlete, gradually moving towards a peak performance. Period five is the main competitive period in which the peak performance will be maintained for the athlete to reach the goals of the season or win a certain competition. Period six is the transition period, which is characterized by a drop in training load, and recovery both psychologically and physically from the competition before the cycle starts again.

More commonly, these phases will be more easily identifiable by being given specific names based on the goals at that point in the periodized plan. It is common for coaches to break up a season into the following periods or macrocycles:

General preparation > hypertrophy > maximum strength > power development > strength/power endurance > maintenance> transition/off-season

The sequence may change but parts of the season will be dedicated to each of the phases at one point or another, typically finishing with the maintenance and transition phases.

The general preparation phase is often the pre-season and may incorporate some of the off-season in some sports. It is often used to get back into training following some time off, or a serious reduction in training load. Gen prep is often non-specific to the sport, but will progressively move towards the requirements of the sport the closer to the end of the phase or start of the season. Often coaches will get the 'miles banked' during the early stages via longer, endurance-based workouts, and will work on sport-specific durations later in this period.

Depending on the needs, there may be a hypertrophy phase to increase the size of the athletes. This phase may be interchanged with maximum strength depending on the needs of the athlete. Often gaining significant levels of strength naturally produces what is termed functional hypertrophy in some athletes without the need for a specific hypertrophy phase.

Following on from the maximum strength phase, coaches will look to develop power. This typically means dropping the number of exercises and performing higher percentages of 1RM or a lower number of reps in order to recruit more fibres, but not exhaust them, in the hope that this will train the recruitment during performances. Once the strength and power levels are created the coaches will look to maintain these values during the important competitions of the season. This is the peak period in which the athletes may only be in the gym twice a week to keep their bodies used to the peak outputs required of their sports.

Within many sports, especially team sports, the in-seasons are often six to eight months in duration, and each fixture is as important as the next in order to win a league or progress through a knockout competition. Often strength coaches will be at odds with the coaching staff during the season because the coaches' goalposts may change depending on how successful or unsuccessful are the teams' performances. This is why the traditional linear model sometimes comes unstuck, especially in the team sports setting.

Undulating models or non-linear models are sometimes used to combat this. The func-

Build Strength

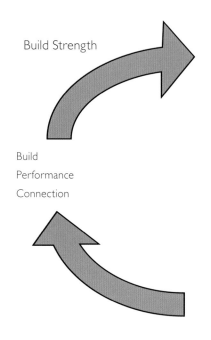

Build Size

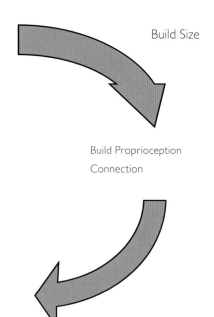

Build
Performance
Connection

Build Proprioception
Connection

tional training system draws from both linear and undulating models.

By separating the movements and selecting different priorities, the programme can be flexible with the coaching teams changing desires while still creating the balanced, functional athletes it aims to do.

For example, if a coach of a soccer team finds a defender is losing the ball regularly due to being pushed off it, the focus of the programme can be moved to enhance the player's upper body push strength without affecting the development of each of the other movement patterns that could be enhancing his game in other areas. Building the upper body push strength will give the player the confidence on the ball to perform his duties better, yet the rest of the programme continues on the regular schedule and all areas are benefiting from what is required at that point in time. In this situation the athlete would have the priority exercise as the bench and increase strength through the 345 schedule

in the foundations template. He or she would still get the benefits of the connection development exercises, and so all-round athletic performance occurs.

The current system will allow you to identify the needs for each movement pattern and then start from the need of the athlete specific to the weakest relative movement pattern.

In the functional training system the exercises will typically follow an undulating cycle of stages, which will repeat weekly to allow for linear progression in those exercises. The cycle follows the priorities discussed previously; creating appropriate foundation strength and size, building coordinated movement (via proprioception), and building the power transfer for performance.

To produce your own programmes, find your starting point for the different movements against the test criteria. Where you are weakest currently for that level will be a priority.

In the example that follows we will assume there is a strength weakness and thus we will take the athlete through the programme looking at one focus point, the squat pattern.

## Categories of the Squat Exercises – Build, Connect and Power

### Exercise Order

Exercise order is very simple. Perform exercises that require the most muscle mass earlier on in the programme. This is why we start with a combination of a couple of the Big

Three or whole body movements in the three stages we outline in this text, building stages and the powerful–performance stage.

Below we outline the template which you can use and the reasoning behind it for both the Building 1: foundations and Building 2: balanced performer, and the in-performance stages: peak power.

## Building Phase 1: Foundations and Function (Fn)

The foundations stage (see Table 6.1) is a highly productive phase that can even benefit some of the more veteran athletes out there. This phase follows an AB workout split. Most athletes new to training will be deficient in their

**Table 6.1 Foundational strength example.**

| | Workout A | Workout B |
|---|---|---|
| Big 3 Strength Section | | |
| A1 | *Back squat* | *Back squat* |
| A2 | Mobility drill | Mobility drill |
| B1 | *Bench* | *DL* |
| B2 | Bent row | Pull-up |
| (B3) | Mobility drill | Dip |
| Connection exercises (focus pattern) | | |
| C1 (Squat/lunge) | Goblet squat | Compass lunges |
| C2 (Upper push) | Press-up | DB bench press |
| C3 (Upper pull) | CTB | One-arm row |
| C4 (Hinge) | Hip bridge | Glute ham raise |
| C5 (Upper vertical push) | Half-kneeling landmine press | DB military press |
| C6 (Upper vertical pull) | BB high pull | Pull-up |
| C7 (Brace/rotate) | Plank circuit | Corkscrew |
| | | |
| Met conditioning | HIIT 4 (5 mins rest) | HIIT 4 (5 mins rest) |

## Profile Case Study

Male basketball athlete in their mid-teens (fifteen years old), can back squat 0.5 bodyweight for ten repetitions (1RM equivalent of 0.67 × bodyweight). Is not especially quick or able to slam dunk, suggesting a poor vertical jump from lack of power in the lower limbs as a result of poor strength previously noted (0.5 bodyweight).

Looking at the lower body level in the squat pattern, we would possibly select the back squat as a starting point as the athlete identifies with this exercise. Over a few weeks, following the functional strength 345 scheme for this exercise we would expect to raise the 10RM (as we have this we would be happy to use this test again as a comparison for the athlete) during the **foundations** programme. This involves the athlete squatting three days a week with increasing loads over the twelve weeks. They will also learn the basic human movements in order to prime their neural systems into being able to connect the strength in performance-like movements.

This phase will allow the athlete to achieve the target range of 0.75–1.0 × bodyweight lift for 1RM for a U15 male athlete, increasing back squat strength by up to 33 per cent, relative to 1RM. So we are now at a level that is acceptable for the athlete's age and now need to get this to be useful within their performance.

Following on from the athlete's foundations phase, the athlete now has the better squat and has more than likely improved their vertical jump as they are able to recruit more muscle fibres from learning how to squat more. However, the athlete still isn't as quick as the coach may like, so we move to the **building a balanced performer** programme and are now looking at helping this individual to develop the ability to use the strength they now possess. The squatting continues in the programme, although heavier lifting is dropped to two days per week, in which one day the squat is the highest priority lift of the day.

On the other day it is a secondary lift but still aiming for a strength or hypertrophic response and may be a front squat or split squat variant. The third squatting action of the week in the programme comes in the connection section of the template. This will work on the athlete using their own bodyweight in the squatting or lunging patterns to replicate a movement that will be performed during a competitive fixture. This may involve a bodyweight distraction such as a band or medicine ball being rotated while squatting or lunging to ensure that the pattern can be stressed and is pliable enough to meet the changing demands of a perform situation, or as the athlete progresses the movement selection will move along the functional continuum and may change to a single leg squat (SLSQ) or pistol squat. These may be performed as a super set (two exercises) or a tri set (three exercises) with exercises selected to develop greater proprioception in the squat pattern, and so these exercises could be, as mentioned before, an SLSQ, developing into a pistol squat, with the 3D squats and also combine some landing in a squat position as some injury reduction technique work. SLSQ/pistol squats will help the athlete to learn to control the squat pattern unilaterally. The 3D squats will teach the body to be able to squat safely with distractions to the technique, increasing injury resilience, and the landings technique is a precursor and injury reduction for the peak performance phase that will move into more explosive exercises, which could include jump squats. This will connect the strength and size from the foundations and build phases, the ability to squat with a distraction in a controlled manner and produce a powerful movement in performances involving a jump and a crossover into acceleration on the court in the **powerful performance** programme.

Over the course of the cycle the athlete may have developed in size, both height and weight, and so the strength level at the end of the foundations programme may now be relatively less (i.e. the athlete puts on 5kg in size in six months and the load now is less relative to body weight). So now we start the cycle again, looking at the back squat being brought up to body weight or even surpass bodyweight (e.g. U18 target range of 1.0–1.5 × bodyweight) and the cycle starts again. However, this time the core strength is lacking to connect the strength of the lower limbs, so we look at adding an overhead squat pattern to the mix, either OH squat in the foundations phase to get that pattern up to a better level, moving the connecting movements into lighter offset BB OH squats, or one-arm overhead squats. This will be done before progressing onto the powerful performance phase, where in the first instance the athlete will look to develop the explosive push press pattern. He or she will also develop the brace exercises and the rotational exercises to build the strength in the torso musculature at the same time.

## What if the Athlete Was Strong to Start with but Weak in the Core?

If the above was the case then we could start with the athlete's first foundations programme focusing on low-load OH squats alongside the rotation and brace movements and build up the coordination and strength of the OH squat to kick-start the connection between the strength the athlete already possessed and the performance that would be expected with those strength levels. The athlete would need to learn the foundation human movements in order to benefit in the build phase from the connective exercises that would progress here. With both of the above scenarios the other areas of the athlete's abilities have been in rotation through various points on the speed-strength graph, and thus have continued to develop in a balanced manner while the weakness catches up. Therefore the athlete is getting more balanced the more times they rotate through the programme, each time addressing the weakest area and still allowing for gains in all the others.

## What if the Coach Picks Up a Weakness Mid-Cycle?

If this happens we can amend the priority exercise or swap from the build back to the foundations phase, correcting the imbalance and resetting the cycle to maximize the performance of the individual athlete. Meanwhile, the athlete's other attributes in the connection levels can remain unaltered as they are also part of the foundations programme and the athlete continues to push on in performance assessments and playing performance.

## % of Competition Speed

| Wk (session) | Wk 1 | Wk 1.2 | Wk 1.3 | Wk 2.1 | Wk 2.2 | Wk 2.3 | Wk 3.1 | Wk 3.2 | Wk 3.3 | Wk 4.1 | Wk 4.2 | Wk 4.3 |
|---|---|---|---|---|---|---|---|---|---|---|---|---|
| of Competition Speed | 70 | 80 | 90 | 75 | 85 | 95 | 80 | 87 | 95 | 80 | 90 | 100 |

Fig. 6.1   Metabolic conditioning development.

squat. Therefore you will squat three times a week, and either bench twice and deadlift once or vice versa on alternating weeks, to build the Big Three exercise strength levels, and perform the basic connection exercises to become proficient in the seven movement patterns. This phase lasts twelve weeks.

Section 1 covers the Big Three strength exercises, Section 2 of the template covers each of the seven movements in which you need to acquire proficiency in order to perform at the top of your game, and Section 3 covers metabolic conditioning. The focus is on gradually building intensity in a linear pattern week to week, but achieving performance level of conditioning rapidly within the programme and maintaining high levels (Int: 75%+) each week.

## Building Phase 2: Building a Balanced Performer (BBP)

Phase 2 has a three-section template, which can be broken down into various subsections. Our first aim is to build either strength or functional hypertrophy. Phase 2 continues with the primary focus on the Big Three; however you will squat and bench twice a week, and deadlift only once rotated through on workouts A, B, and C. From the template section below you can see that each of the Big Three takes the priority on one of the workouts. This phase lasts between six and twelve weeks depending on the competition calendar of the athlete.

As you can see, the template exhibited above has A1 and A2. You will use this for the Big Three lifts: A1 will be the big lift, A2, a supplementary exercise or mobility exercise that may or may not complement the big lift in AI. If it does complement it, it is to improve or groove the pattern or partial pattern of the big lift. In the case of the horizontal press, we pair this up with the horizontal pull because you can develop a more balanced approach to adding weight when they are matched up (you should be able to pull what you can press).

The next group of lifts are labelled B1–3. This is the time in which we can focus strength onto a movement that has not yet been performed. It may be further along the functional continuum but is still a build-ing exercise and, as you can see, there is some replication of the Big Three within this subsection, although never on the same day. This means we can train the horizontal press and the squat patterns twice a week without performing while fatigued. As you can see in Workout A, the horizontal press and pull are in exercise slots B1 and B2 with an optional mobility drill in B3. You can go heavy in the horizontal press without it having a lasting effect on Workout Cs AI and A2. The squat/ lunge pattern in Workout C makes the case for the same and is only ordered differently because we are also looking to add a brace or rotation exercise into the build section.

**Table 6.2 Building balanced performers template.**

| | Workout | | | Olympic Learning Cycle Example |
|---|---|---|---|---|
| | **A** | **B** | **C** | |
| **A1** | Back squat | Deadlift | Bench | Bench |
| **A2** | T-spine mobility | Glute mobility stretch | Horizontal pull – CTB | Horizontal pull |
| | | | | |
| **B1** | Bench | BB lunge | Back squat | OH squat |
| **B2** | Horizontal pull | Compass lunges | SL step-up | Snatch grip high pull |
| **(B3)** | Mobility drill | X | Mobility drill | YTWs |
| | | | | |
| **C1 (C1)** | V. press – BW dip | V. press – DSOHP | V. press – mil press | V.Press – BW dip |
| **C2 (C2)** | V. pull – pull-up | V. Pull – DB/KB high pull | V.Pull – one. arm DB snatch | V. pull –pull-up |
| **C3 (C3)** | Hip hinge – SL RDLs | Brace – corkscrew | Hip hinge – GHR | Hip hinge – SL RDLs |
| **C4 (D1)** | Lunge – 3D lunges | Squat – SL step up | Lunge – ankle mobility | Lunge – 3D lunges |
| **C5 (D2)** | Brace – anti-rotation press | Lunge (power) – Heidens | Brace – wall Xs | Brace – anti-rotation press |
| | | | | |
| **Metabolic Conditioning** | HIIT/GRID | HIIT/GRID | HIIT/GRID | HIIT/GRID |

NB If you require a learning phase for the Olympic lifts then B1 may be the overhead component of the lift and B2 the second pull, e.g. B1 – push press variant and B2 – high pull. If this is required follow the Olympic progressions in the relevant positions.

The next section is where we are focusing on developing the connection between the strength we have gained and the movement efficiencies we have introduced in the foundations phase. This phase can be perform either in a circuit of C1–C5, or can be split into a tri set (three exercises) and a super set (two exercises). Either way is up to you, although if you need a quicker workout rotating through C1–5 cuts some time off the total. As they are

**Table 6.3  Powerful performance phase template.**

| Exercise | | | | A | B |
|---|---|---|---|---|---|
| Circuit 1 | Reps | Sets | Load | Upper | Lower |
| **POW1 – Heavy Explosive Power** | 3+3 30sec rest between 3 sec | 5 sets | 10RM | BB push | BB high pull |
| **Heavy Loaded** | 2–3 | 5 sets | 4RM | BB mil press | Deadlift |
| **POW2 – Optimal Loaded Power** | 8–10 | 5 sets | 30–60% of 1RM | BB push jerk | Hang clean |
| **Max Speed – BW/Low Load Exercise** | 5–10 | 5 sets | BW – 30% of 1RM | Med ball wall | Box jumps |
| | | | | | |
| Circuit 2 | Reps | Sets | Load | Upper | Lower |
| **POW1 – Heavy Explosive Power** | 3≠3 30s rest between 3s | 5 sets | 10RM | Bench | SL step-up |
| **Heavy Loaded (>90%1RM)** | 2–3 | 5 sets | 4RM | One-arm DB bench press | Reverse lunge |
| **POW2 – Optimal Loaded Power** | 8–10 | 5 sets | 30–60% of 1RM | ½ kneeling cable press | DB triple exit |
| **Max Speed – BW/Low Load Exercise** | 5–10 | 5 sets | BW – 30% of 1RM | One-arm med ball throw | Heiden |
| | | | | | |
| **Metabolic Conditioning** | 6 | 3 sets | Max effort | HIIT sprints | HIIT sprints |

lower loads the rest time between exercises is low and the focus on different areas allows for a semi-continuous circuit, providing you have all the equipment around you, without being that hoarder in the corner of the gym.

The final section is the metabolic conditioning section. This is a way of creating some short bursts of intensity, increasing the metabolic cost of the workout, then enduring this more throughout the phase and adding in more specific conditioning for your sport. If you have multiple team sessions and fixtures during the training week feel free to miss out the metabolic conditioning work.

## Powerful Performance Phase (PP)

The PP phase reverts back to an AB split or workouts; however, they are set up very differently. In this phase we are looking to maintain our maximum strength and peak for a competition or period of the season during which it is important to perform well. The workouts have an upper body and lower body component, which alternate in priority. In either case they have the following outline. The exercises are grouped into a four-exercise rotation, sometimes called a giant set.

We aim to hit multiple points on the speed-strength curve over the four exercises. This phase lasts four weeks.

The first exercise is our heavy explosive power routine. This is aimed at recruiting as many motor units as possible to create the connection with performing lower threshold exercise with the larger amounts of motor units. This exercise is at the top range of the optimal load for the exercises used. It is also performed as a split set with a thirty-second break between to increase the number of reps completed in a short period of time.

Next is the heavy loaded exercise (>90% 1RM), this is to further stimulate the recruitment of high threshold fibres. This will be performed for 1–4 reps before progressing onto the optimal loaded power exercise (POW2). This will allow the over-recruited fibres to play a part in the force production for the optimally loaded exercise.

The final exercise is a body weight exercise (with potential to add up to 30% 1RM load in very strong athletes); this focus is on the speed end of the speed-strength curve. This ordering will hopefully develop a PAP response, an increase in performance output, and a learned higher threshold recruitment response from the muscles in the future.

CHAPTER 7

# FUNCTIONAL EXERCISES

The Big Three, as they are often referred to, as seen as the biggest 'bang for your buck' exercises. They recruit large numbers of fibres in the working muscles groups, recruit the bulk of the major muscle units of the body and have been repeatedly shown to sustain the improvements in performance gains for beginner and intermediate lifters for many years.

The Big Three moves are the squat, deadlift and bench press.

These three exercises can be game-changers when a level of performance is above a certain level. Each can add to different athletic skills in a way another cannot. Equally, there are limitations to sticking to only these three exercises as they do not all follow into the functional philosophy. They can all be progressed and regressed adequately enough for all abili-ties to be able to perform a variation of the Big Three, whether new to the training game or an elite athlete. These lifts will be part of the programme, but will be rotated with other exercises to increase its functionality. These movements are deemed Priority level I lifts. They give the biggest return on invest-ment out of almost any exercise, and at least one movement should be performed in each workout.

## The Back Squat

The most common squat is the barbell back squat. The bar is placed across the shoulders and sits in the groove created by the trape-zius and the spine of the scapula. This groove can be made more prominent by pushing the

**COACHING BOX**

The squat allows the body as a whole to create stabilizing structures and movements at the same time. It primarily works on the ability to work within the triple extension and triple flexion of the ankle, knee and hip.

The triple extension is an important movement for us in which to perform daily tasks. From standing, to walking and running, the triple extension can be used at varying intensities, in many different situations throughout the day.

It is essential to running, jumping, lunging and squatting, and all variations of those.

There are many other squats, including the barbell front squat, barbell overhead squat, Zercher squat, sumo squat, split squats and variants, body weight, squats with alternative weighting, e.g. kettlebells, dumb-bells, medicine balls and many other weighted objects.

**Table 7.1   The squat continuum.**

| Type of Exercise | Leg press | Smith machine squat | Barbell | One-leg squat | One-leg squat on instability pad |
|---|---|---|---|---|---|
|  |  |  |  |  |  |

elbows back with a 90-degree elbow, as seen below:

# Five Benefits of Squatting

- Strengthens core, hip, back and lower limb musculature
- Increases coordination at hip and knee
- Recruits large mass of muscle in a sporting movement pattern
- Allows a large load to be controlled in a key human movement pattern
- Is a base movement that strongly crosses over into sporting movements

### RATE OF FORCE DEVELOPMENT

Rate of force development is a measure of the amount of change in force over time as force is produced. It is typically measured as newtons per second, or newton-metres per second.

# The Deadlift

Strictly speaking, the deadlift is the movement of the load from stationary on the floor to a standing position. Traditionally this was performed with the bar moving straight up in front of the legs and the legs only got straighter as the lift progressed. Fifty to sixty years ago saw the introduction of the double knee bend, which allowed a) greater loads to be lifted, and b) a biomechanical advantage to be made in the mid-point of the lift, by allowing the lifter to use more muscle mass. This can be a contentious issue on the worldwide web; however, I feel that the technique of the double knee bend within the deadlift is a result of naturally wanting to produce the greatest rate of force development, thus is a suitable technique to promote crossover into sporting actions and sporting training programmes that incorporate the Olympic lifts.

The deadlift incorporates the posterior chain musculature, or the glutes, hamstrings and erector spinae of the back. These muscles are also those used to take the stress in the squat. So why use another exercise in the Big Three that recruits the same musculature? Is one not covering those? In essence, no. The relationship between the bar and the centre of gravity is different. The forward lean in the deadlift is a necessity, whereas in the squat it is a technical faux pas. This is because of the mechanical stresses placed on the lower back when the bar is above the torso. Incidentally, this is part of the reasoning as to why we do not coach the barbell good morning at any level; the second reason is for the lack of opportunity for a safe failure in the good morning exercise, leaving the athlete in a vulnerable position.

The other difference in the technicalities of the deadlift allows for a greater recruitment of the upper back muscles not required in the squat other than as a passive resting place. The active recruitment of these muscles in the deadlift acts to prevent the rounding of the shoulders during the lift and maintain the slight curve in the lumbar spine. As a result, the lats, rhomboids, trapezius, rear deltoids and spinal erectors are all engaged within the deadlift, unlike in the squat.

Looking through internet articles, books and blog posts, you can find every tip, variation, pro, con and technical efficiency for the deadlift and why one style is better for one person than another. Others will simply 'grip and pip' with little regard for technical finesse. The following sits in the middle of the cloud of information that is the deadlift. It promotes a slight knee bent position in the RDL for reps technique, although this will not necessarily occur in deadlifts from the floor.

## The Silverback Gorilla

This is how we set up for a deadlift, by getting into our gorilla position. The silverback gorilla is an easy image to visualize for many people: the broad-shouldered hanging arms, hips low to the ground, back angled, chest puffed out with pride position is synonymous with the image of the ape.

1. The chin is between a tucked and neutral neck position. Tucking the chin or preventing the excessively extended position prevents a mechanism called the extensor reflex occurring. This reflex creates signals in the body to arch the spine, sending the hips forwards, leading to anterior pelvic tilt, which prevents the glute group from contracting optimally via reduced recruitment. The extra anterior pelvic tilt also causes excessive lordosis, which is definitely not what is required during a deadlift. It has been noted that those loading through excessive lordosis are at a higher risk of displacing the discs anteriorly within the spine, what is known as slipping a disc anteriorly or towards the front.

2. The chest is held high with the shoulders back – pinching the shoulder blades is a coaching cue that can create stability in the upper back prior to the lift.

3. The hands are gripping the bar just outside shoulder width. Multiple grip options are available: under hand, over hand or mixed. Often the bar will roll out of under hand and over hand unless straps are being

*Fig. 7.1 The strength of the deadlift set-up can be compared to nature's own silverback gorilla. 1. tucked and neutral; 2. high chest; 3. shoulder width; 4. natural back curve; 5. feet hop width apart.* (Photo: Wikimedia Commons)

59

used and so for beginner lifters I would use a mixed grip; that is one hand over and one hand under, which prevents the bar rolling one way or the other.

4. The curvature of the back is slight but is maintained throughout the whole lift.

5. The lifter is crouched with the knees within shoulder width, ideally placed at hip width, toes pointed forwards and the bar over the first or second eyelets of their shoes.

From this position it is pretty simple – you stand up. However, there is an art to standing up with a load from the SBG position, this art comes in the form of correct sequencing to economize the movement pattern, recruit

the most muscle fibres and pose the least threat to the body's structures in terms of injury. These are explained in the relevant exercise technique section.

## Differences for the Ectomorphically Challenged

Those of you cursed with long femurs and arms and short bodies are especially at a

Fig. 7.2   Deadlift start and finish positions.

disadvantage in the traditional deadlift. It is common to see ectomorphic lifters 'hip kick' as they perform the deadlift. The hip kick is a result of the hips lying so far behind the bar they are all but rendered useless, or very difficult to recruit at least, and so the go-to guy is the quads. Using these to extend the knee maintains the hips in the poor position as the bar is lifted, which increases the danger of shearing forces affecting the lumbar region.

Typically the ectomorphic lifter experiences lack of flexibility in the hamstring, hips and calves. Each cause a disturbance to the deadlift pattern. Tight hamstrings lead to posterior pelvic tilt, resulting in a rounded lumbar spine and rendering the erector spinae pretty useless in the extended position. Tight hips prevent the ability to reach

*Fig. 7.3   Sumo deadlift start and finish positions.*

the depth to lift the bar from the floor, as do tight calves, and so the torso compensates by creating more forward lean, increasing the risk on the lumbar spine. So I think it's safe to say that flexibility work is a must for the ectomorphic lifters out there, but what changes can be implemented now to allow these guys to deadlift while their flexibility issues are hammered out? A few options are available and are equipment-dependent.

The first is to change the loads position relative to the hips to allow for greater involvement from them. This can be done via two variations of the lift requiring different equipment needs. The first is the trap bar deadlift. These pieces of equipment are becoming more readily available in fitness suites around the world and are also being manufactured for home gyms with a relatively low-cost, entry-level bar available in most places. The trap bar has a parallel grip configuration, which means that the load is beside the lifter rather than in front of him or her, reducing the amount of forward lean necessary during the lift and producing a more upright position to lift from.

The alternative parallel gripped deadlift is the dumb-bell (DB) deadlift. Often this exercise is limited by the size of the DBs on offer to provide adequate loading for adaptation to occur. If completed from the floor, the DB deadlift requires greater flexibility and so is troublesome for ectomorphic lifters. Lifting blocks can help in this area of deficiency.

The other alternative is the sumo deadlift. This lift requires a wide stance, leading to the feet pointing out significantly. This stance has the benefit of drawing the hips closer to the bar, producing the more upright position comfortable for ectomorphs due to the reduced contribution of the lower back in supporting the load. During this lift the bar should maintain a position close to the body of the lifter.

# The Bench

The main test, often seen as THE test of strength for many gym-goers. Although there is little transfer of the movement pattern to standing sports, the strength base that can be created for upper body pushing ability warrants its inclusion in many programmes.

I want to make sure that as you read up on this technique you are aware of its position on the functional continuum. In the continuum presented previously it is the second-least functional exercise for the horizontal press, second to the machine press variation. There are other exercise variations that could be included into the continuum that may displace the position of the exercises presented; however this book is not an encyclopedia of most to least functional exercises. If it is such a disfunctional exercise why include it? The bench press can be used to create a strong upper body, and coordinate force development through the core and hips. It is often forgotten that the bench press in the traditional variation of the technique requires the planting of the feet on the floor, and so the ability to transfer the forces put into the floor up through the hips and core and into the upper body is also important.

### Getting it Right from the Start

If you lift the bar from the rack and just hope for your body to do the right thing within the movement then you're lifting without a purpose. The bench is a very technical lift that when performed correctly is a dream; perform it poorly and you're looking for trouble. Getting the starting position right is critical, and there are a few parts to preparing the lift. So what grip should you use (over hand, under hand, alternate, hooked or non-hooked?), what width should you grip the bar (narrow, medium or wide?) where should

your elbows be during the lift? (close, perpendicular, midway between the two?) Should you incline, decline or flat bench? Will I hit all aspects of the pectoral muscles if I only perform one bench variation? In response to the last question, the amount of research looking into muscle activation of the pectorals in various positions, equipment and hand position has yielded support for everything and nothing. Focus on building the strength levels that are adequate and then on how you can apply them and you'll see the benefits of lifting the way it is outlined here, and the simple changes that can create the neural adaptations to occur for optimal performance.

## Pros and Pitfalls in Traditional Bench Press Technique

The masters of the bench are the powerlifters. They perform seriously impressive scores on the bench and because of their supremacy on this equipment they have been used as the template for performing the bench for years. However, not all of us are gifted with short arms and big barrel-like chests to shorten the distance travelled by the bar to be judged enough for a competition lift. In body building circles many lifters cycle the grips to better target specific muscles so they have more stimulus to 'grow'. If they wish for the pectorals to 'grow' then a close grip will be used. In the majority of the population the close grip, slightly outside of shoulder width, is less than useful for athletes and non-bodybuilder gym-goers, and here is why; compressing the lift into this position reduces the amount of muscles used within the lift. It focuses the strain on the pectoral muscles while minimizing the use of the anterior (front) deltoids and the triceps. Great for increasing the stimulus for growth of the pectorals, but useless for functional programming. It also has a biomechanical dysfunction inherent in this method of lifting.

The outside shoulder width grip requires the elbows to be flared, which brings a reduction of the space between the head of the humerus and the prominent bony structure that is the acromion process. If you repeatedly reduce this space positionally, yet actively grow the muscles around the space, the ligamentous and tendonous structures are

Fig. 7.4  Different grips and set-ups can affect the load and the repetitions you can perform but have varying adaptational benefits.

compressed further into the space, the space quickly runs out and this leads to shoulder impingement issues, which often lead to time away from training.

Commonly, health care professionals suggest time away from training to allow inflammation to die down, which it does. Muscle atrophy also occurs in some prolonged absences and so the impingement disappears. Training resumes and progress is steady until the impingement occurs again, and so the cycle repeats until something breaks: the will of the lifter to train, or the structures in the shoulder.

It is not a surprise to see the findings of Raske and Norlin (2002) showing power-lifters' most prominent injuries are in the shoulder, with an incidence of 0.51 per 1,000 hours, and the difference over a number of years showed increases in this injury, which I presume to be a result of more lifters copying the techniques that dispose the lifter to the shoulder impingement issues outlined earlier.

For many lifters, simply bringing the hands to shoulder width, in a closer but not close grip position, will increase the space between the humeral head and the acromion process. It may also mean that the bar is lowered to a position further down the ribcage than traditional bench technique calls for. This is better for the functional lifter due to the increase in activation of the anterior deltoids and the triceps adding to the lift, and will increase the ability to connect the movement in a sporting position due to more muscles being involved.

The maximum you can lift on the bench press can also help to calculate the amount you can lift in other exercises without trial and error. Mike Boyes suggested the figures for converting your 1RM bench press into incline and dumb-bell variations. Table 7.2 provides these figures to the nearest load on standard equipment. This will be useful to calculate loads of the exercises that will be rotated through to provide training stimuli in a variety of positions, angles and stability challenges. This rotation will allow for greater functionality and crossover in the horizontal press to sporting performances and actions.

Increasing an athlete's lift in one area will lead to a benefit in another of the lifts, i.e. increasing loading on the DB Incline from

**Table 7.2 Bench press conversion table – useful if you haven't access to a barbell or are performing supplementary exercises.**

| Exercise | Max Bench Press | Incline Bench | DB Bench (5RM) | Dumb-bell Incline (5RM) |
|---|---|---|---|---|
| **Load** | 100% | 80% 1RM max bench | 64% 1RM bench (divide by 2 for DB weight) | 80% of DB bench (DB weight) |
| | 120kg | 95kg | 37.5kg/DB | 30kg/DB |
| | 100kg | 80kg | 32.5kg*/DB | 25kg/DB |
| | 80kg | 65kg | 25kg/DB | 20kg/DB |
| | 60kg | 47.5kg | 20kg*/DB | 15kg/DB |

*rounded up to nearest common load available, this may result in 4RM load rather than 5RM.

25kg for sets of five to 27.5kg for sets of five, your bench press will increase to 107.4kg from 100kg previously. Having this mentality will allow you to keep training fresh, varied and allow you to keep punching through training plateaus.

## Session Preparation

### Warm-Up Sequences

Within our warm-up protocol we have a series of drills that are aimed at doing as many roles as a warm-up requires in a short space of time as is practical. Whatever the goal or sport you are training for you can benefit from many aspects of the warm-up series, individually and as set out here. The warm-up begins with some foam rolling, into mobility work and into specific warm-up for the activity to follow. Outlined here is the generic section of the warm-up. Following on from this would be some drills suited to the activity you are about to undertake. For example, following on from this in a rugby setting we will run through some sprint drills over short distance, then add in change of direction components and some contact preparation work. In most cases readers will be looking to perform a gym session and so the specific warm-up work to follow is the barbell warm-up. If an athlete has a specific injury history such as ankle trauma we may also include some proprioceptive stimulation for the lower limbs.

### Self Myofascial Release

Myofascial release (MFR) is a technique that has come to the forefront in gyms and facilities around the world in the last five to ten years mainly through the use of foam rollers. Myo indicates areas of muscular involvement in the technique, while *fascia* relates to a white connective tissue that surrounds our cells, organs and muscle structures. It is fibrous in nature yet very elastic. It changes density depending on its whereabouts, superficial or deep. Fascia forms a connection from each cell, organ or muscle structure to every other cell, organ or muscle structure in the body.

The concept of MFR is to realign the muscle and fascia components towards their original optimal state. It is easiest to think of the muscle cells as building blocks. Ideally they should be in neat rows (fibres), this allows them to work optimally as each row can shorten and lengthen appropriately.

When multiple rows of muscle suffer trauma in the form of heavy resistance training, direct impact, or micro tears during activity, the rows sometimes twist and no longer are aligned in their perfect rows. In fact it is more of the case that the rows have twisted, coiled and tangled at the point of trauma. These points are quite gristle-like, sometimes referred to as knots, or trigger points. The rows around them now use these points as an anchorage; however these rows are now shorter than optimal. As the muscle is worked more, or sustains more trauma, the tangled mass draws in the cells directly next in line and grows bigger, again shortening the muscle row length. As you can no doubt appreciate, this is not allowing the muscle to regain optimal performance, rather making it worse.

Within these tangled rows the by-products of energy conversion, congealed blood, and other waste products such as dead white blood cells, get caught and essentially solidify. These by-products have no way of escape, creating a toxic mixture that sits waiting for a release.

During MFR we must release this toxic cocktail to realign the muscle fibres and regain the fibre length. It is a necessary evil to release the chemicals in the knot and as such should be prepared for. Essentially this toxin will work its way into the bloodstream and eventually be passed as urine. To reduce the effect of these toxins, ensure good hydration and adequate salt intake.

## Fascia Bands

Fascia gets described in many ways in which to understand a theory on its purpose within the body. One of the most useful ideas we use is the idea that there are eight bands of fascia that may interconnect at times, thus creating a connection with every other cell, organ and muscle structure within the body. These eight bands are places on the anterior and posterior of the body and guide us in our movement pattern understanding.

Two bands at left and right run from the top of the head to the end of the toes, running down the neck, chest, abdominals, hip flexors, quads, tibialis anterior and into the toe extensors. The mirror bands run the opposite way down the back, through the neck, lats, erector spinae, glutes, hamstrings, calves and follow the Achilles tendon under the foot to the end of the toes.

The diagonal bands run from the tip of the left fingers, up the arm, through the left pectorals, into the opposite abdominals and obliques on the right-hand side, right hip flexors, quads, and down to the end of the toes, with the same happening from the right hand to the left foot. The position bands run up the arm, through the lats, into the quadratus lumborum (QLs) on the opposite side, through the glutes and down to the underside of the foot and to the toes once more, again on both diagonals across the body.

This knowledge is important in order to understand the areas and directions in which we foam roll.

## Self MFR

Self MFR starts with the feet. Either barefoot or in socks is required, along with a ball that provides pressure when the foot is pressing on it. Rolling the ball around the foot allows the fascia to be manipulated and increase in temperature and therefore elasticity. Pockets of gristle-like structures may be found at various points when looking to work the fascia. Aim to roll across the whole foot, especially in the gristle-like areas, for thirty to sixty seconds each foot. NB: If you are short on time in the gym we recommend the feet are released prior to a gym session as we have found that this triggers many of the patterns we require firing, although a thorough warm-up is preferred.

From here we move on to the foam roller, a piece of equipment made of formed foam that is cylindrical. There are many on the market with various gimmicks added but a simple foam roller is good enough for the warm-up purposes here.

Starting from the Achilles tendon and working up in 15cm sections, we work our way up the fascia lines towards the top of the head. We are looking for the gristle-like, knotted sections to focus on.

When working on the calves, rotate your feet from pointing to the right to the left and back again. The calves have fibres that are not perfectly straight and so will benefit from the angular changes here, as will other areas of the body. When the knots are found there are three ways in which to release them.

Personal preferences dictate how you will deal with these points:

- The first is to remain perfectly on the spot, squashing the knot apart. This is very direct and may feel similar to a manual therapist performing a trigger point release on the knotted area.
- The second is to roll from an area above or below the knot and try to break down the edges of the knot with each approach.
- The third is to run from the top to the bottom of the area causing the discomfort.

No one way is superior to another, it is purely personal preference so experiment with all three. You may find some areas you prefer one technique over another.

From the calves we move on to the lower section of the hamstrings, again rotating our feet to cover the three hamstring muscles; biceps femoris, semitendinosus and semi-membranosus, from the lateral aspect of the legs to the medial. You should move up after

Fig.7.5   MFR foam rolling sequence.

ten seconds of rolling that elicits little resistance, or more if you uncover knots to work on.

From the hamstrings we move on to the glutes. The glutes are actually orientated to pull at a slight angle across the hip. And so a shift in position is required to hit the glutes with appropriate MFR. We have found sitting with the knees slightly flexed and placing the outside of one ankle on the opposite knee opens up the glutes on the side where the foot is lifted, so by rotating onto that glute you can create a similar angle of attack to begin rolling. Switching feet and the side you are leaning towards allows each glute to be released individually.

Moving into the lower back: the QLs, erector spinae and multifidus muscles require a little balance and torso recruitment. For the lower portion you may be able to use the elbow on the floor to provide support while working the roller up and down. Once in the mid-section of the spine it is easier to balance on the roller. In the upper back we come across the lats, another muscle in which line of pull changes the rolling direction. Again we can roll towards the side you are targeting and ensure the pressure moves from the mid-spine towards the shoulder on each side. However, we also encounter the scapulae, which move depending on our arm position. So it is only fitting that once the lats are released we work on the muscles that get stretched and/or exposed when we move the scapulae around.

Some athletes will work on the back of the neck as well. However, foam rollers may be too cumbersome to get into the right areas. If you find it difficult to reach a point that you feel needs some attention, move on to a tennis ball, cricket or lacrosse ball, or if you're really sadistic a golf ball. If the foam roller is too soft for an athlete we have been known to use a piece of (clean, unused) downpipe. It has been

rumoured some elite athletes venture to serious levels of exploration in MFR, with some even using rolling pins!

From the top of the back we turn over and roll out the quads. Those with tight Achilles may wish to target the T quads, and tibialis anterior too before hitting the quads. Many athletes will bend at the knee to lengthen the quad musculature and allow the release to hit deeper, as well as rotating the feet from one side to the other. Many athletes in foot-striking sports such as soccer, rugby and martial arts find a fair amount of gristle just above the knee. Remember, it is important to roll out these knots so that the muscle can function properly. Again, maintain the 15cm sections as you move up the thigh into the hip flexors.

At the hip flexors we recommend using the roller towards the tip of one end. This allows the opposite hip to rotate down and the roller to get into the medial aspects of the hip flexors. Try also to extend the hips forwards during this section.

The abdominal region proves difficult to isolate due to the organs behind the muscles, and so we skip to the pectorals. Again the tip of the roller is useful in getting into the pectorals as you approach the shoulder. Work the roller from the sternum towards the shoulders at roughly 45 degrees to release the muscle in the correct line of pull.

The final area is the IT band, which runs from the outside of the knee to the hip; think of the stripes commonly found on tracksuit pants and follow that. This structure is a bit of a mishmash of muscle and tendon. It is prone to knotting and so can be the most sensitive area to roll out. If a physio or trainer has performed a modified Thomas test on you, you may know that your IT band is tight if when relaxed your leg veers away from the centre line.

Remember, self-MFR can optimize the muscles and fascia to work better, providing a better working environment and recruitment process of the body. As you start to identify with these points you can speed up on the areas that don't need as much work and focus on the trouble spots. In some athletes it is reported to add 5kg to a lift, with up to 2.5kg just from rolling the ball around the foot.

# Warm-up Mobility Sequence

The warm-up sequence covers the human movements and takes inspiration from various practitioners, including Mike Boyle, Mike Robertson and others.

## High Knee Walks

To start with we work on the **high knee walk**. This is where on each step taken the non-weight-bearing knee is drawn to the chest, the hips are extended and a tall posture is maintained throughout. If balance allows we will also ask the athletes to rise up on their toes on each step.

This stretches the hip flexors on the weight-bearing limb and the glutes on the non-weight-bearing limb, and does so in a controlled action relating to higher-speed running. The action requires coordination to be performed accurately, agility and balance to maintain the tall posture and change of limb directions under control. By rising up onto the toes we further the active recruitment of more muscle fibres by recruiting the opposite hip flexor to pull the knee closer.

Athletes suffering with lack of mobility of the hips may want to use the modified high knee walk. The athlete takes hold of the shin on the inside of the leg and draws the ankle to the belt buckle, allowing the knee to fall outwards. By using a double handgrip of the shin you can maintain posture and prevent hunching over the leg, as hunching will restrict the arm on the same side as the lifted leg.

## Lunging

From the high knee walks we move into the **lunge** pattern, of which there are a number of variants to use. In the standard forward lunge you are looking for a mid-length step to allow both knees to flex to around 90 degrees. Keeping the shoulders above the hips, the chest is kept high and a neutral spine is encouraged. The rear foot pushes forwards and the front foot is controlling and decelerating the movement. For some the challenges of this are enough to complete around 30m or thirty lunges going forwards. Stepping backwards into a lunge (reverse lunge) increases the percentage of gluteal muscle recruitment by up to 5 per cent in some studies.

For those who may at some point in their sport back pedal, or run backwards, a **reverse lunge** is encouraged to promote balance and coordination, with the added stimuli of not knowing what is behind. Often people will struggle more as they are not familiar in this pattern. A common mistake is to have a slight forward lean to compensate the backwards travel. Work hard to maintain the upright position.

Athletes prone to tight hip flexors, and those who are in a seated position most of the day – read office workers, students, etc – may benefit from the **lunge with over-head reach**. This can be performed as per a regular forward lunge or as a reverse lunge. Both or single arm variants are equally useful; however each can add a little extra.

## Lunge with One-Arm OH Reach

The arm opposite the leading (most forward) leg, is raised laterally overhead, and this creates a stretch within the hip crease musculature on the raised arm side. This stretch can be increased further with a lateral lean to the leading leg's side.

Fig. 7.6 Mobility warm-up sequence. 1a and 1b. high knee walks; 2a and 2b. lunges; 3. lunges with one-arm over-head reach; 4. lunges with two-arm over-head reach; 5. single-leg deadlift walks; 6a and 6b. squat stands; 7a and 7b. T-spine rotations.

## Lunge with Two-Arm OH Reach

Both arms are raised anteriorly to an overhead position. This reduces the stretch effect in the trailing legs hip but extends the ribcage and torso musculature.

In both of these variations the scapula is required to move to reach the positions of OH arms and so a little preparation is also targeted into the shoulder structures.

## Lunge with Rotation

The lower limbs part of the lunge is performed as any other lunge. In the stepping part of the sequence the shoulders are rotated towards the front leg. Sometimes it helps to be holding an object such as a bar, hockey/lacrosse stick, rugby ball, medicine ball, or clasp hands together. Aim to maintain the shoulder height level throughout the rotation. This movement, after a little practice, will become more fluid and less of two separate actions [lunge and twist] so that the rotation occurs during the downward phase of the lunge whether forward or reverse lunges are performed.

All of the lunge variations act to stretch out the hip flexors, and wake up the rest of the leg musculature in preparation for the work to be done in the session.

## Single Leg Deadlift Walks

To warm up the hip hinge pattern and increase proprioceptive drive or the balance maintenance system, we next perform the **SLDL walk**. This movement actively stretches the hamstring before contracting the posterior chain muscles to bring the torso upright once again. Maintaining a flat back throughout is often a challenge. The rear leg that is lifted behind the weight-bearing foot can be straight or bent to be used as a counterbalance. The athlete is expected to achieve a horizontal body position with a slight knee bend in the support leg before returning to upright and swinging the non-weight-bearing leg through to take a forward step. Again, this action can be used while walking forwards and backwards.

For those struggling with balance, in the first few weeks of the training they can be allowed to leave the trailing foot's toes touching the ground to create a proprioceptive feedback point before progressing into the full SLDL walks.

## Squat Stands

With feet outside hip width apart, bend the knees, grab hold of the toes and straighten the legs. The hamstrings in most people will become stretched before the legs are straight. Returning the hips to between the feet releases the stretch before being repeated. The top of the stretch can be held for six to ten seconds if lengthening of the muscles is required, or just one or two seconds if used in the warm-up.

If you have tight upper body or poor shoulder range, the **squat stands with OH reach** can be a valuable addition to the warm-up in place of regular squat stands.

The squat stand is performed as above. On each return to the bottom position alternate arms are lifted to extend overhead (see Fig. 7.6) before another squat stand is performed and the other arm is raised. This stretch allows the body to programme the OH position when in a deep squatted position, and also helps to release the T-spine from the tightly bunched position found in many who are desk- or chair-bound throughout the day. This is especially useful in preparation for OH squats in barbell workouts.

## T-spine Rotations

Finally, the thoracic spine rotations complete the basic warm-up protocol. In a bent over but flat-backed position the arms are allowed to hang. Taking one hand and raising it laterally to the floor in this bent over position and

## Table 7.3 Basic warm-up protocols.

| Basic | To Increase Hip Flexibility |
|---|---|
| **High knee walks – 30m** | High knee walk with external rotation |
| **Lunges 15m followed by reverse lunges for 15m** | Lunges with rotation |
| **Reverse lunges with rotation SLDL walks 30m** | SLDL walks |
| **Squat stands** | Squat stands with OH reach |
| **T-spine rotations** | T-spine rotations |

watching your thumb the whole way around allows your thoracic region to rotate while your lumbar spine can be maintained.

### Barbell Warm-Up

Following on from the basic warm-up will be the warm-up that is specific to your main session. In this case the gym work will incorporate some form of barbell work or pattern covered within the barbell warm-up. More technical details are available on each of these movements later on and should be read before commencing the programme.

First up is the unloaded bar front squat. This can be performed with a crossover grip or in the clean catch position.

The main focus is to get moving with the bar in the front squat position, working on the basic mechanics of the squat. The heels remain in contact with the floor as you descend into the bottom position. The bottom position is where the thighs break parallel, the torso remains upright, and elbows are held high to keep the bar on the front of the deltoids. The key to this lift is to sit back into the lift and get used to the change in weight distribution through the feet.

Move the bar onto your back and now perform the back squats to warm up with an unloaded bar. Again we are looking for thighs below parallel, chest up and elbows back to lock the bar into position on its shelf.

From here the bar is moved into a hang clean position to start the unloaded bar RDL. The bar travels down in the vertical plane, staying close to the legs, while the hips move back and upwards to create a stretch in the hamstrings. The shoulders are pulled back to help maintain a strong flat-back position. The bar should end up below knee height while creating the stretch; the knees can be softened to release tension in the lower back. Pushing the hips forwards returns the body to upright and the bar to the hang position.

Moving now into bent over rows, we are aiming for a back position parallel to the floor, similar to the bottom position achieved in the RDL but this time we maintain this position for the number of reps in the warm-up. Draw the bar to the lower ribs and control it back to the extended arms position. The torso must be held strong, the shoulder blades are required to retract and pinch together and the hands are drawn to the lower ribs.

The final move in the barbell warm-up is the vertical press. The exercise in the main programme will determine how the vertical push is prepared for. For those just 'gyming-it' or in sports not requiring much overhead action, you may use the push press with or without a bounce. In the push press the bar is in the front squat position (not crossover grip) and is pushed overhead, ensuring your chin gets out of the way before the head is thrust forward to finish with the crown of your head underneath the bar at the top locked out position. A reversal of the movement under control returns the bar to the front of the shoulders to start another rep.

*Fig. 7.7   Universal athletic position (UAP).*

## Universal Athletic Position (UAP)

Those in explosive sports may wish to adopt the jerk. This involves an explosive movement from the UAP while the feet move in the sagittal plane one foot forwards and the other backwards. This technique is outlined in more detail later in this chapter, but can also be added into a warm-up for learning and repetition purposes.

*Fig. 7.8   Barbell warm-up sequence.*

*Fig. 7.8  Barbell warm-up sequence continued.*

## In Programme Mobility Exercises/Drills

This is not flexibility training! Mobility drills are not about simply increasing the range of motion during a static stretch as flexibility training aims to do. Mobility training is concerned with combining the range of motion in which you can achieve alongside stability in those ranges in order to have safe movement.

Stability requires strength and rate of force development, and thus mobility training is active, not passive like flexibility training. It also tends to be closed chain movement actions where the muscles can react and prevent unwanted ranges to be allowed to develop without the required strength to decelerate the movement effectively and without injury.

## Ankle Drills

### 3D Calf mobs

Many will know of the standard calf stretch, whereby you take a long stride placing the hands high on a wall in front of you in order to create a 45 degree angle at the ankle.

However, this does not cover the range of fibre directions from the muscles joining at the Achilles tendon.

Taking a wide step within the stride at 30–45 degrees from the planted foot will move the feeling of the stretch from a high central position to a lower one, outside the mid-calf. With these two moves we cover more fibre directions and therefore can aid mobility around the ankle. Yet we can cover more fibres still by taking the front non-weight-bearing foot across the body and stretching the medial or inner calf musculature.

Fig. 7.9   3D Calf mobility drill.

# Hip Drills

## Hurdler Mobility

Start on all fours and bring one foot up and close to the opposite knee, preferably in front of the knee. Sit back towards the non-supported side. The hands are kept out in front and in contact with the ground and the rear leg will naturally want to slide backwards and straighten. The hips are returned and pushed forwards without compromising the stretched position. Repeat on the opposite side. This mobility exercise works the TFL gluteus medius and minimus by encouraging them to activate and control the external rotation occurring at the hip joint.

## IR Knee Drops

Lie on your back, feet wide apart but flat on the floor, knees bent. The knees are then allowed to fall gently into the middle space between the legs. Return to upright and allow the opposite knee to fall into the space. The internal rotation allows range of movement development within the piriformis and gluteus maximus due to their elongated position.

## Open/Closed Gates

Walk while bringing the knee up and then externally rotate the hip. Allow the knee to drop and return the foot to the floor. Repeat on the opposite leg. Actively work the psoas and gluteus maximus, and also the stabilizing muscles in the lumbar region.

Fig. 7.10   Internal rotation (IR) knee drops.

Fig. 7.11   Open/closed gates mobility drill.

Fig. 7.11  Open/closed gates mobility drill continued.

Reversing the direction of this drill allows the 'closing of the gate'.

## Walkouts

These can be performed in a number of ways. The traditional way, and the reason they are also known as inch worms in some places, is to start in a standing position, feet as close to each other as will allow you to touch the floor with the palms of the hands. The athlete reaches down and walks the hands 'inch by inch' away from the feet until in the extended press-up position.

We also want the athlete to dip the hips to the ground in a back extension position, before walking the feet 'inch by inch' up to the hands.

If space is limited you can walk out and back with the hands or perform one worm, hands out and feet in, then stand, turn around and repeat. Whichever way you choose will develop hamstring length, hip coordination and a connected torso. These can also be used as a brace movement pattern exercise that is often prescribed in the five to twelve reps range.

Fig. 7.12  Walkouts.

# Thoracic Spine (T-spine) Drills

## T-spine Rotations

The T-spine rotation exercise is the same exercise as in the warm-up (see Fig. 7.8). It can be used within pairings to complement an exercise or ensure the warm-up of this region has not worn off. To recap, performing this movement involves a start position where the back is flat and the shoulders are in front of the hips, the arms are allowed to hang and shoulders clear the knees. Taking the working hand and raising it laterally to the floor in this bent over position, allowing the upper spine to rotate within an axis of itself and watching your thumb all the way around allows your thoracic region to rotate while your lumbar spine can be maintained, leading to greater thoracic mobility while protecting the vulnerable lumbar region.

Fig. 7.13   T-spine start and finish.

## T-spine Wall Mobs

These are an easy and effective thoracic extension developer. You require a flat vertical surface in which you can place your forearms and have enough space to not be impeded by any equipment or wall fixings.

Place the forearms, from hands to elbow, flat against the wall around shoulder height. The feet are shoulder-width apart and behind the shoulders. As the knees are flexed the chest is pushed towards the wall, while the lumbar spine and hips maintain the relative position to the feet, as shown in Fig. 7.14. Work hard not to flex the lumbar region and allow the T-spine to perform the exercise. Return to the start position. Breathing out on each lowering into the wall mobs can help so long as the lumbar spine does not take over in extending the spine.

Fig. 7.14    T-spine wall mobility start and finish.

## T-spine Compass

This drill is more about understanding the position of the upper torso in relation to the rest of the body. In can be used effectively within individualized warm-ups, if the training times allow, or can be used in a superset with another exercise.

Standing upright, the sternum and lower ribs are pushed forwards and upwards to extend the T-spine into the 'north point of the compass'. When reversed it becomes the southern point.

Lifting one side of the ribs and shoulders will take the T-spine laterally, and both sides complete the east and west points.

## Wall X

The wall Xs are a way of identifying whether or not you have sufficient rotational ability in the T-spine. An optimal X would be both feet touching and pointing in the same direction along the wall, hips outward facing, with both palms flat on the wall and the shoulders facing the wall. Many people will get into the position with the feet a foot or more away from the wall with ease. It is the narrowing of the gap between the feet and the wall that changes the ability to functionally rotate with the T-spine.

Fig. 7.15    Wall X stretch.

79

## Shoulder Drills

### Cheer Bands

Using a resistance band, the athlete stands upright, with their arms straight in front of them at shoulder height. The direction of pull with straight arms is between 20 and 45 degrees and its opposite. The hands return to the middle before the opposite direction is performed. Following both diagonals, the hands return to the start position and then pull horizontally. All three movements make up the cheer band exercise.

Fig. 7.16   Cheer bands drill.

## Pullbacks

Again this uses the resistance band, tethered to a rail or non-moving object. The hands are to be drawn from an extended in front position to past the hips at the back, maintaining an upright torso position and not extending the hip to reach the shoulder extension required. These two points contribute to the majority of incorrect form on this exercise to give the illusion that the arms are being drawn backwards when in fact the hips are brought forwards in incorrect form.

*Fig. 7.17   Pull backs.*

## YTWs

YTWs relate to the shapes created by the athlete while completing this circuit in a prone position. It is a way of developing scapular control by creating the body's understanding of the arms in relation to the shoulder and torso. The movements in these shapes include scapular retraction and/or elevation of the scapula. This circuit can be progressed in a number of ways. Firstly, you can start on a flat bench and perform the YTWs, moving onto a glute ham raise device that will require more torso tension to maintain a straight line, or a stability ball/gym ball, which requires balance in multiple directions. You may also wish to progress with low loads if the athlete requires strong shoulders.

## Floor/Wall Slides

This exercise and progression is best started on the floor. Feet are allowed to be in a sit-up start position and the backs of the hands are placed on the floor, level with the head. The elbows should also be in contact with the floor. The hands are then moved to a position on the floor 'above' the head. They are then moved to below head level. Throughout

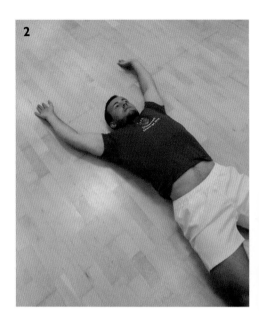

Fig. 7.18   Floor slides.

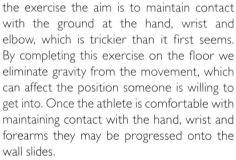

the exercise the aim is to maintain contact with the ground at the hand, wrist and elbow, which is trickier than it first seems. By completing this exercise on the floor we eliminate gravity from the movement, which can affect the position someone is willing to get into. Once the athlete is comfortable with maintaining contact with the hand, wrist and forearms they may be progressed onto the wall slides.

These differ in that they are performed in an upright position. The hips are also to maintain contact with the wall and you are to prevent over-arching the lumbar spine. The arm movement remains constant.

It is often difficult to maintain the contact and so where you can achieve this, work on increasing this range over a period of time. Adding it into daily stretches is a good way of creating shoulder mobility quickly.

## Brazilian Curls

I was first introduced to this move by coach Nick G in Newcastle, England. Essentially it encompasses multidirectional, multi-planar movements with varying muscle tension requirements. As a whole movement it can look complicated but broken down into stages is easier to learn and progress from.

**Stage 1:** Cross-body biceps curl: This creates internal rotation at the shoulder while the biceps are working concentrically.

**Stage 2:** Scarf test: The elbow is taken overhead and the hand moves over the shoulder to end in a position at the nape of the neck. The rotator cuff has a highly complex patterning here in which movement transitions between multiple planes and axis.

**Stage 3:** Triceps extension: The hand is lifted above the head. The triceps are now the concentrically active muscles, while shoulder stabilizers are also active.

*Fig. 7.19   Brazilian curls sequence.*

**Stage 4:** Adduction of the arm back to the start position. The deltoids and trapezius muscles now work eccentrically to control the movement.

This move can be performed alternately on each side or can be completed for a number of reps on one side before attention turns to the other.

# Exercise Progressions Library

## 'Rules to Progress'

1. *Move with correct mechanics*
   Ensure the body starts and ends in the correct positions and that the segments move in the way they should for that movement.
2. *Move within alignment*
   Maintain the neutral spine, neutral head posture, weight distribution.
3. *Technique*
   Perform what is being asked, not just shifting the load from A to B. It must be proficient for it to be beneficial long-term.
4. *Timing sequencing of a movement*
   Get the order of the technical components right and with correct sequencing.

In order to achieve all of these points we must execute the seven patterns, whether within the Big Three or supplemental lifts to feed into the seven movements, with greater frequency, build more intensity over time while striving to progress the skill before progressing or evolving the action along the functional continuum.

All exercises can and should be manipulated in one of, or multiples of, the following ways:

I   Altering the base of support
II  Altering the lever arm – e.g. adding weights or equipment
III Increasing Range of Motion (RoM)
IV  Altering the speed an exercise is performed – NB increasing and decreasing can be a progression. Think eccentrics
V   Adding a distraction
VI  Manipulating the planes of movement

## Movement Priorities

The aim of the programme is to work within everyone's abilities, experience and timescales. With so many factors in life as to when we are available to train, such as work and family commitments and geographical proximity to facilities, the ability to train with purpose can be restricted. This is the reason why we have three levels into which the movements fit when producing programmes. As a general rule, we will always have a Level 1 and some form of Level 2 exercise within a workout. It may be that you have less time to complete a workout; you may be late to the gym or trying to squeeze a session in at lunch, so you can only manage a couple of exercises and some mobility work. Therefore we need to have the most effective builders of strength and/or hypertrophy exercises within this short time. Below is an overview of the conditions of each level.

**Level 1** – These are the Big Three movements: squat, press and hinge. This does not mean that only the back squat, bench and modified deadlift will be used, but that a squat pattern, a press either vertical or horizontal and a hinge pattern will be completed. By using one or two of these movements in a workout you hit the biggest groups of muscles and therefore with the right stimuli can create the greatest training effect. For example, a strength-focused workout of two major exercises may contain the front squat and a mobility drill, and a vertical press such as the military press and mobility drill. By including these big movements in the example exercises above, we perform eccentric (lengthening) loading of the hamstrings and the concentric (shortening) phase for the quads group. This creates stimulus for strength gains. A braced position of the core is created due to the upright and front-loaded bar in the front squat and further increases the core recruitment during the overhead push of the military press, further increasing strength gains. A strong core allows greater force transfer in the concentric action of the triceps and upper back muscles. This would be a time-effective workout, however, and is not suggested to be a staple in your programme.

**Level 2** – Although some programmes only use the Big Three, I have found that incorporating counter-actions to those in Level 1 to prevent imbalances are particularly productive to building an athlete. These typically will be pulling and hip extension movements and are strength- and power endurance-focused. You will often rotate through the connection exercises of the remaining seven movements not covered in Level 1.

The vertical upper body push and pull, horizontal pull, lunges, bracing and rotation are all covered. The selected exercises feature throughout the programme, due to the focus and current need of the athlete. Level 3 exercises are often pushing for a greater proprioceptive focus, often with roots to develop the strength exercises of the Level 1 and 2 exercises, but can be under lower loads or body weight challenges.

**Level 3** exercises are used for developing power and for crossover into the sporting arena. They can vary in the loads used but typically work involving torso rotation and transfer of forces through the torso in a metabolic conditioning style takes precedence.

NB: most functional does not mean can be loaded the most!

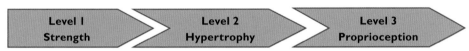

Fig. 7.20   The three stages of developing an exercise

## Squat Patterns

### Back Squat
This is the primary lift of our foundations phase. It recruits a large amount of muscle mass, produces the highest hormonal response for building strength and size, and is a great way of mapping your progress for transfer to your sport due to the triple extension pattern the back employs.

Fig. 7.21   Squat sequence front facing and sideways on.

Fig. 7.21   Squat sequence front facing and sideways on continued.

*Fig. 7.21    Squat sequence continued.*

### Start Position

Set up the bar inside the squat rack with an appropriate height of safety braces. The bar should start around 2 to 4in below shoulder height and collars should be used. The feet are positioned in line with the hips and are centred under the bar. The feet can be positioned at a comfortable width, between hip- and shoulder-width apart, with the toes anywhere between 10 to 2 and straight ahead (see Fig. 7.21).

The bar is grasped outside of shoulder width, creating around a 90 degree angle at the elbow. This will depend on the athlete's preference for a comfortable grip and positioning of the bar, and does not need to be too prescriptive. From this position the athlete is able to create a shelf for the bar to rest upon by pushing the elbows back and retracting the shoulders. The chest should be held high and proud, the abdominals braced, and a neutral head and spine position should be engaged.

### Eccentric lowering of the bar

The preparation for the lift continues with the athlete performing the Valsalva manoeuvre;

this is the taking in of a deep breath, filling the torso with air, and squeezing around this in order to create a solid mid-section. This manoeuvre takes the strain from the erector group and saves the shearing forces from being applied to the vertebrae, reducing the chance of injury. The feet are corrected in the central position under the bar with the weight directed through the centre. Triple simultaneous flexion of the hip, knees and ankles starts the bar's descent under control. During this lowering of the bar, the knees are kept in a position that allows for them to track over the toes, following the angle of the foot direction.

The thighs are to break parallel in order to ensure a full range of movement. The weight distribution has now shifted through to the front of the heel. As with the starting position, the chest should be held high, the abdominals braced, and a neutral head and spine position should be engaged.

### Concentric lifting of bar

Once depth is achieved the upward or concentric phase of the lift to return to standing is achieved by the explosive triple extension of the hip, knee and ankle. During this phase the weight moves from the front of the heels back to the centre of the feet. At the top of the lift the athlete can breathe out as the column of gases has completed its role in securing the torso at the bottom of the lift.

---

**COACHING POINTS**

- Shoulders and elbows back with tension in the torso
- Deep breath before lowering to protect the spine
- Aim for an explosive lift even when lifting heavier.

---

The bar can then be racked after the desired number of repetitions.

## Squat Sitting

To get used to the position, athletes can perform the squat sit. This is where the athlete lowers themselves into the bottom position of the squat and holds this position. Often the athlete will use a squat rack to maintain balance and keep their focus on the bottom position, not on trying to stay standing. The important thing here is to maintain the neutral spine and that knees are tracking over the toes.

*Fig. 7.22   Butterfly squats mobility drill.*

## Butterfly Squats

These are similar to the squat sits, but they are performed under the athlete's own balance. The elbows are placed inside the knees, and the hands are placed palm-to-palm in a prayer-like manner. The hands are then pushed down to push the elbows outwards to create the range of motion at the hip so the athlete can squat deeper.

## Deep Squat Overhead Press (DSOHP)

*Fig. 7.23  Deep squat overhead press or Sotts press.*

(See mobility work but expand on developing strength.)

The iron back exercise as it was introduced to me. This little exercise can bring the big boys to their knees. It has crossed over into our programmes from the weight-lifting arena and in some circles is called the Sotts press.

The athlete starts in a deep squatted position. The bar is racked, as it would be in a back squat. Once at the bottom of the squat the athlete presses the bar up over their heads. The athlete will normally experience a tightening of the erector spinae muscles and multifidus across the mid-back, especially after a number of reps have been performed. Each press is one rep and there is no change to the athlete's position in the deep-squatted position throughout the set. Once

the set is completed the athlete can then stand up.

Starting with a broomstick and moving up in 1kg increments is adequate for steady weekly progress in this exercise over the course of three to six months.

**Table 7.4  Squat game-changing targets.**

|  | Game-Changer Squat Scores |
|---|---|
| Adult male | 1.5–2 × BW |
| U18 male | 1.25–1.5 × BW |
| U15 male | 0.75–1.25 × BW |
| Adult female | 1.0–1.5 × BW |
| U18 female | 0.75–1.0 × BW |
| U15 female | 0.5–0.75 × BW |

## Front Squat

Front squat technique does not differ greatly from the back squat. The main difference is the positioning of the bar, which alters the centre of gravity. However, the front squat starting position, or racked position, is important in many other exercises and the development of functional athleticism requires the ability to perform a range of exercises such as the push press and push jerk. It is also instrumental in learning the clean catch position in order to progress to the clean in the power exercises.

The bar is placed across the front of the shoulders and sits in the groove created by the anterior deltoids slightly above the clavicle (collarbone). This groove can be made more secure in holding the bar by pushing the elbows higher than shoulder height; this locks the bar into place, as in Fig. 7.24.

The front squat increases the torso musculature firing, stabilizing spinal movements and creating a strong torso as a result. Some internet sites will say it also places greater stress on the quads, and therefore to build bigger quads you require this exercise. We are more interested in its role in developing strength in the torso and its carry-over to the clean. The front squat racked position is also important in the development of shoulder flexibility.

We believe that if we are to clean, push press and jerk, we need to be comfortable in the front-racked position. As many have diffi-culty in this position we have a drill (elbow touches, see below) in order to improve our racking of the bar. We also prescribe that the athlete should attempt the best front-racked position they can, either by getting the elbow up and the bar in the groove, or by the use of lifting straps being loosely looped and the athlete gripping the tail ends as close to the bar as is comfortable. This provides the athlete with enough repetitions of racking the bar to be comfortable when he or she does eventually have the range of movement to achieve the required position, speeding up the transition into the clean derivatives.

**FIVE BENEFITS OF SQUATTING**

- Strengthens torso musculature, hip, back and lower limb musculature
- Increases coordination at hip and knee
- Recruits large mass of muscle in a sporting movement pattern
- Allows a large load to be controlled in a key human movement pattern
- Transfers into Olympic lifts

*Fig. 7.24   Front squat sequence.*

# Drills to Develop Front Squat Technique

## Wall Squats

Many athletes struggle to be comfortable in the upright posture of the front squat, while their hips and torso are behind the base of support. It is common to have athletes falling forwards, resulting in two issues: posture and safety. Posturally, the back becomes rounded and the elbows end up below the shoulders, allowing the bar more freedom to escape the control of the athlete. The knees track far beyond the safe zones of the toes, leading to increased shearing forces that are furthered by the lack of depth associated with this fault.

With the potential for injury and lack of bar control it is important for athletes to address the posture and depth issues as this will tend to aid in the safety of the lift. An exercise to develop the posture in both the front and back squatting techniques is to stand with the toes an inch from a wall. You then squat and the wall prevents the knees tracking beyond the safe zone of the toes. Therefore, in order to get more depth the athlete is required to let the hips sit back. The wall also prevents excessive forward lean due to the close proximity of the athlete's face to the wall. By performing this drill the athlete will ingrain the pattern required and the confidence to sit back into the squat will develop rapidly.

## Elbow Touches

This drill is used when the posture is good but the athlete is struggling to lock the bar in place. This can be due to long forearms, or more often a lack of range of motion at the shoulder, which is often caused by tightness in the rotator cuff combined with rounded shoulders. If the athlete shows rounding of the shoulders this must be addressed before the front squat position will be comfortable. However, if it is tightness in the shoulders this is often due to the body being wary of a new position and putting up protection in case there is injury potential. What you need to

Fig. 7.25   Elbow raises/touches mobility drill.

do is bypass and re-educate the body that the new position is safe so it will drop the barriers.

To do this we rack the bar in the front squat top position. We then find the furthest point that can be reached by the elbows together. Then in turn we move each elbow 2in beyond that point a number of times, six to twelve reps per elbow. This is followed by doing six to twelve more with both elbows together.

What we have done is show the body it is safe for each individual elbow to go beyond the barrier point, therefore when you return to both elbows you can go further. Repeating this a couple of times can dramatically alter the forearm angle during the front squat. It can take weeks to reprogramme the new ranges as permanent changes. However, it is worthwhile in the end, as the amount of load you are comfortable racking on the front squat will increase rapidly, as will your performance.

Fig. 7.26　Overhead (OH) squat start and finish.

## Strength Targets

Front squat technique once learned should allow for greater than 80 per cent IRM back squat load to be performed in the front squat at all ages once technical competence has occurred.

## Overhead Squat

By taking loads overhead we move the load further from the pivot point or fulcrum. In doing so we increase the effort required to overcome the inertia at the further distance. In the case of moving the load overhead, the load (the external weight) is further from the fulcrum (the torso), thus requiring the torso to recruit more muscles to prevent unwanted movement or, worse, injury to the spinal structures. Therefore by progressing overhead lifts from low loads and increasing session by session, week by week, we can develop strong torso musculature that protects the spine, and the posture of the athletes.

The overhead position to start the squat is with a close-grip snatch or roughly shoulder-width grip. The bar maintains a position over the crown of the scalp at the back of the head, the shoulders are back, and the lumbar spine slightly arched. This position dictates that the posture throughout the lift will remain as upright, if not more upright, than in the front squat. The lower portion of the body still follows the same rules as the previous techniques in the squat; sitting back into the squat, weight transferred from mid-foot to the heel and back to the mid- and forefoot. The thighs are expected to break parallel with the ground and the heels are to remain in contact throughout.

## Benefits of OH squats
- Increased torso development
- Increased muscle recruitment of the torso
- Ability to deal with loads away from the body

# Drills

## Offset Loading

One way we can develop the OH squat without adding excessive loads is to offset load. This is to load one side with a weight different to the other, creating torque forces – forces to act around a pivot. As mentioned before, this would be the torso musculature in this instance. Offset loading can be achieved by loading a barbell differently at either end or using different dumb-bells or even different types of weights, e.g. a dumb-bell and a kettle-bell. We would only advise variations of up to 2.5kg on a barbell and only once the athlete can OH squat 75 per cent of their own body-weight.

**Table 7.5   Offset loading recommendations.**

| Adult | =<2.5kg |
|---|---|
| U18 | 1.25–2.5kg overload |
| U15 | 1.25kg overload |

## Single Leg Squat Patterns

It is not often within the sporting world that athletes are required to have both feet in ground contact while performing sports skills. Athletes are more likely to be in locomotion than with both feet planted. This is part of the reasoning behind the cycling of exercises and the movement along the functional continuum as we see it. By adding in the single limb exercises, we increase the specificity to sporting actions and create instability. This increases neural drive, proprioceptive demand and the stabilizing action of the pelvic musculature, specifically gluteus medius and quadratus lumborum's role in providing stability during single leg stances. It is also interesting to note that many rehabilitators are identifying single leg exercises as key to the rehabilitation process and knee prehabilitation programmes aimed at injury prevention and reduction.

It is our opinion that absolute strength that can be developed in double leg exercises, however integral to a performance programme, is required to be progressed from the building phase to developing the connection within the athlete's sporting context.

These exercises should first be mastered with only the athlete's body weight over a number of sessions, over a period of weeks in order to ingrain the technique and develop the ability to correct balance. By increasing the repetitions by one or two reps each session up to fifteen the athlete can benefit in a number of training variables before external loads (bars, dumb-bells or weight vests) are added to the equation. We can then further progress by moving into explosive jumping movements in many of the single leg exercises, which allows for increased muscle fibre recruitment and coordination and increased recruitment of stabilizing patterns in the landing phases. This also aids better crossover into explosive sporting actions such as sprinting, as well as increasing proficiency in controlling deceleration actions such as cutting and stopping.

## Split Squat

The split squat is the absolute starting point of single leg squat patterns. By starting in a lunge stance, one foot forwards of the other, we provide a wide and stable ground contact point. (Note that the feet remain in place throughout the whole set; the exercise does not involve the movement of either foot forwards or backwards as in the lunge pattern described later.) The rear knee is then lowered to the floor by flexing the front

Fig. 7.27    Split squat.

leg and maintaining the front knee above the front foot. Maintain an upright posture, keep the shoulders back.

This exercise can be developed by raising the back foot on aerobic steps or a bench and can be loaded with a barbell or dumb-bell in either the front or back squat positions. This exercise also develops hip flexor muscles and the athlete can often feel the development of the stretch.

## Overhead Split Squat

As with the split squat, the feet remain in place. The external load, most often a studio bar or barbell, is held in the overhead position with a close-grip snatch position and the arms locked. By doing so we add in flexibility development at the shoulder as well as the hip flexors, and this improves posture through the extension of the thoracic region. This variation provides a time-efficient exercise that works the single leg squat pattern and improves flexibility in both hips and shoulders.

Again, this exercise can be developed in the same way as the standard split squat.

## Pistol or One-Leg Box Squat

This single leg exercise is perfect for developing balance as well as single leg strength. It can be difficult to work the movement pattern for many people during the early attempts. However, perseverance in performing this will allow the athlete to reap the rewards come game time.

The non-working leg is used to counterbalance the change in weight distribution during the exercise; the arms can also deliver this function. The hips are lowered to the block under control. If easier, use some extra weight in the hands to help with the counterbalance. While the squat pattern is developing it is easy to try to lift the heel to develop the range required to get down to thigh parallel. (Lifting the first toe helps keep the weight

Fig. 7.28    Pistol squat and skater squat.

bearing towards the heel.) This prevents the movement starting at the ankle and keeps the focus on the musculature at the knee and the hip stabilizers.

## Skater Squat

This variation of the one-legged squat is ideal for those sports in which the body is compressed into a less than desirable position. It is ideal in grappling-type sports as it simulates a defensive rear leg position that does not contribute to the action of driving the front leg. In the exercise technique, the rear leg and the arms can serve as counterbalance measures, or can be progressed to adding a distraction. (i) A rotation element can easily be added to this exercise with the help of a resistance band, in a Pallof press skater squat hybrid exercise. (ii) An alternative distraction for the working leg involves wrapping the resistance band around the knee to add the lateral resistance either medially or laterally (iii).

## 3D Squats

This exercise is great for connecting the lower body and the torso with very different upper body actions. The 3D squats involve three different upper body actions while performing a squat as normal with the lower body. The first is a squat with overhead raise. The ideal action is to start in a stand-

ing position, arms relaxed with the bar at hip level. As you squat down the hands holding the broom or studio bar rise at the same rate as you lower, finishing above the head as you sit deep (below parallel) into the squat.

Fig. 7.29  3D squats; varying movement within a squat allows transfer of the coordination of the squat into less orthodox positions within your sport.

The second action involves a rotation, from the standing start position, bar out at shoulder height. As you squat down the shoulders are rotated one way, while the hips are aiming to stay straight so that the rotation comes from the T-spine rather than the lumbar spine. Depth is as deep as normal, below parallel.

The third and final part of the 3D squat involves the athlete starting with the bar in the overhead position. As the squat develops the athlete leans to one side and this move causes the centre of gravity to shift, creating the difficulty. Often athletes will try to be quick in the lean to prevent unbalancing; however the slower the better the connection between the torso and the dissociated lower limbs.

## Jump Landings

Most jumping involves an element of plyometric activity. Plyometrics often receive bad press or stipulate specific strength requirements before adding them into programmes. However, understanding that we perform many plyometric activities naturally in our daily lives shows that we are capable of loading our lower bodies without much training history. If you are mindful of the process of developing the ability to land better you can reduce the likelihood of injury. The stages of jump landings can be developed from two starting points.

To reduce the forces placed on the joints and structures during landing the simplest exercise is the jump onto a box. From the ground you are required to make the jump up to the box. As some momentum is still in the vertical plane the feet will be allowed to make a softer landing, therefore the forces are reduced.

Another drill that requires a partner is the variable foot landing position drill. This can be developed with height off a step, over an object, or with a 180-degree jump into the landing. The process is the same. As the athlete jumps into the air the partner uses his or her hands to symbolize the foot position they want the athlete to land in. The positions can be as varied as the partner can think of; however the following hand and foot positions show many of the standard options.

(i)   Shoulder width
(ii)  Narrow
(iii) Wide
(iv)  Right forward Left back
(v)   Wide diagonally opposite
(vi)  Left foot only landing

The single foot landing is the final stage of landing ability. It requires the most stabilization from the pelvic muscles as well as increasing the forces within the structures of the lower limb.

## Hip Hinge Continuum

Many of the issues surrounding hamstring injury are a result of training the hamstrings for the purposes of solely flexing the knee. However, the hamstrings cross two joints, the knee and the hip. Thus if we only train the hamstrings in the knee flexion pattern we are leaving the hip extension pattern severely under-equipped. One of the most important functions of the hamstrings is to control the deceleration of knee extension during the sprinting/running cycle. It is also a muscle that is required to work when various portions are doing the opposite of the preferred action, e.g. the knee is flexed and the hamstring is still expected to work as a hip extensor, or vice versa. This approach to the hamstrings is not from anatomy texts and lectures; this is about considering the real function of the muscles during exercise. However, this approach has led to <1 injury: 5,000 hours to the hamstring group among those trained by the author.

# Deadlifting

Start from the silverback gorilla position outlined in the Big Three overview section earlier. The athlete performs the lift from the ground or from blocks to aid in the technical competence in the lift.

## First Pull

To stand up the lifter should aim to raise the bar from the floor, keeping their shoulders over the bar, while maintaining the same back angle of the hips to shoulders in relation to the floor. The path of the bar remains constant; it goes up, vertically. This part of the lift is traditionally the slowest part. Although slow, it is performed with the intent of getting the load off the floor as quickly as possible.

## Transition

Once the bar is around knee height, the lifter's shoulders may come up quickly, while the hips are simultaneously driven forwards to reach the UAP. The change in the body angle, the movement around the knee and reaching the UAP is known as the transition of the lift.

*Fig. 7.30   Deadlift – first pull phase.*

*Fig. 7.31   Deadlift – transition phase.*

97

## The Second Pull

Once in the UAP the lifter is now in a position to increase the muscle recruitment to finish the lift in a standing position. In terms of weight distribution in the feet, it is described as the weight normally moving into the heels at this point. Some lifters find the weight moving backwards offputting but the correct finish position is a slightly backwards lean, and

*Fig. 7.32   Deadlift – the second pull.*

a straight line from heel to shoulders. I like to see the lift finished properly with a shrug; this just creates habit for when the athlete/lifter moves into the Olympic lifts.

## RDL

The RDL is a way of performing the deadlift pattern quickly, while protecting the back due to the pressure being released from the erector muscles owing to the softening of the knees associated with the technique.

With the RDL you lift the bar from the ground or a low racked position and get to a standing, fully extended position. The knees are softened with a slight bend to around 15 degrees. From here the hips move backwards as the weight distribution moves from mid foot to the heel. The bar is to follow a vertical path during the hips being pushed backwards. Once the hips are back and the weight is just above knee height, the athlete should push the hips upwards; this will intensify the feeling or work in the hamstrings. The bottom position is when the hips have been driven back and up and the bar hangs slightly below knee height. The athlete then returns to the standing position by forcing the hips forwards and finishes with a shoulder shrug, as with the regular deadlift pattern.

**Table 7.6   Game-changing deadlift scores.**

|  | Game-Changer DL Scores |
|---|---|
| Adult male | 2.0 × BW |
| U18 male | 1.5 × BW |
| U15 male | 1.0 × BW |
| Adult female | 1.5+ × BW |
| U18 female | 1.0–1.5 × BW |
| U15 female | 0.75–1.0 × BW |

## Glute–Ham Raise

The Glute–Ham Raise (GHR) is a strength- and hypertrophy-based exercise that teaches, especially beginners, to use the hamstrings as hip extensors rather than knee flexors. The many variations to the equipment used to perform GHRs shows that the understanding or focus of each machine differs slightly, but still develops the glutes and hamstrings as hip extensors. Some of these machines are even mounted on the wall in some facilities to accentuate the loading during the extended isometric portion of the exercise. It has been suggested the ability to hold various pos-

*Fig. 7.33    Glute–ham raise.*

itions isometrically throughout this exercise may reduce the likelihood of hamstring strain injuries. The reports are primarily anecdotal; however, there could be some merit in the principle. Therefore we suggest alternating between sessions of isometric holds, building up to ten to twenty seconds at fully extended (0 degrees) and at 30, 60 and 90 degrees of hip flexion, and dynamic exercise will cover the bases for increasing localized isometric strength and the transfer of this strength into performance.

## Trap-Bar Deadlift

The trap-bar deadlift is a great alternative for many athletes over a conventional deadlift. The construction of the bar allows for the load to be in line with the body. The technical difficulties of maintaining a close relationship with the shins is removed and the athlete starts in a more upright sitting posture, reducing the likelihood of injury to the lower body.

To perform the trap-bar deadlift, the athlete steps into the hexagonal space and grips the handles, which are orientated in a neutral hand position. The athlete is then required to simply stand up with the bar. This bar can also be used to perform other deadlift variations.

## One-Leg RDL

The one-leg RDL really focuses on the stability of the working hip. To perform it the athlete is required to stand on one foot, flex at the hip maintaining a neutral spine position and use the non-weight-bearing leg as a counterbalance. The torso, via flexing at the hip, is drawn level with the floor, creating a stretch in the hamstrings. A return to standing completes the exercise. This can be developed by adding dumb-bells, which can aid balance and also increase the strength unilaterally in each portion of the posterior chain.

The exercise forces the recruitment of the hip stabilizers; however it is common for athletes to rotate the opposite hip upwards to reach the range of motion expected in this movement. The simple fix for this is to internally rotate the non-working leg. We have found that this corrects the majority of one-leg RDL compensations at the hip.

## 3D RDL Touches

Similar in nature to the 3D squats, we are looking to encourage stability in three planes of motion during this exercise. The first we have our athletes become comfortable with is the sagittal plane RDL touch. A body-weight RDL is performed but the change is that the athlete stands away from a wall or target point on a squat stand or similar so that when reaching for it during the exercise it is at the end of their comfort range. This exercise can be developed through speed of execution. Attempting it more slowly can increase the time and effort required by the proprioception mechanisms, thus increasing difficulty. Fast movement can also increase the difficulty due to the need for stabilizing muscles to work quicker, but also the increased speed reduces the proprioceptive demands, decreasing the difficulty. Once the athlete is comfortable with the distance from the target, increase this by around 2cm the next time. Always

Fig. 7.34   3D RDL touches.

work at the edge of your comfort range, as this is where change is affected and positive performance changes can occur.

The second plane of movement we expose is the frontal or lateral plane. The athlete stands side-on to the wall or target, on the foot closest to the wall. Again the reach should be at the end of the comfortable range. A slight SLSQ is allowed during the exercise to alter the centre of gravity and help the athlete reach laterally to the target. This can be developed by increasing the distance from the wall, and also by changing the standing leg to the leg furthest from the wall, which changes the challenge of the movement completely.

The third plane is the transverse plane. This focuses on the rotational element and dissociation of the upper and lower hemispheres of the body. The athlete is still required to stand on one foot. However, this time the athlete stands with his or her back to wall. The two options are to use the same arm and leg and rotate to touch the wall behind, the other is opposite arm to leg. Both these movements can be split again to touch on the same side as the arm or cross over the body. Each has a different challenging aspect and all should be covered across a connection phase to be fully functional in producing an injury-resilient athlete. To load this pattern more heavily once mastery has occurred the touches may be loaded with medicine ball to create a hybrid exercise of part MB wood chop/lift with the single leg rotation wall touch.

## BB Hip Bridge Thrusts

This is an extension of the traditional 'core' exercise of the body weight hip bridge. This exercise enlists the external resistance from a studio bar, EZ bar or barbell. (If these are not available, kettlebells, dumb-bells or plates can be used instead.) The starting position depends on the athlete's level of comfort.

Ideally, the shoulders should be placed on a bench or aerobics step. The athlete is sat on the floor with the barbell in the hip crease and the feet in a strong flat position in which to drive through. By driving into the feet and raising the hips to level with the shoulders, lifting the barbell in an explosive action, we develop the hip extension pattern. Slowly lowering the bar develops strength due to this eccentrically loading the hip extensors. Adding plates and focusing on explosive concentric action and slow controlled eccentric action, we build strength and power within the two actions of the exercise. If no load can be added then the traditional bridge raise can be substituted.

## Hip Bridge Development

Hip bridges are a regression of the BB hip thrusts. This is a Pilates-type move that is used for teaching the BB hip thrust and for creating the connection for stabilizers if strength is not the weakness in the torso and hip junction. To perform, the athlete lies on his or her back with feet flat on the floor, hip-width apart and brought close to their glutes. Driving into

the heels increases the glute group involvement. The finish position is the hip and knee in a straight alignment, shoulders on the floor taking the weight.

To increase the difficulty there are a number of different approaches. One main alteration is to affect the base of support; however in this position there are two solid bases: the shoulders and the feet. To change the shoulder base you need to reduce the contact of this area with the floor. To do this you can either cross the arms across the chest or hold the arms vertical. Lying on a roller or ball will also develop this in terms of reducing the shoulders' base of support; this can also include a gym ball under the shoulders.

For the base of support at the feet, simply placing the feet closer together will achieve this in the first instance. The closer together, the less stable. The next step is to take one foot off the ground into the one-leg hip bridge.

Note that we do not encourage the gym ball bridge via the feet due to the position the neck is placed in when this exercise is performed. There are many other alternatives to developing unstable bases so we feel it unnecessary to place the neck in a compromising position.

*Fig. 7.35   Hip bridges: standard foot placement and narrow foot placement.*

## Press Patterns

Pressing and some pulling patterns can be modified differently to other exercises. We can alter the stance, which can affect balance, but can also change the kinetic chain contrib-

uting to the force produced. There is no standard starting position; however we may identify a weakness in technique that will allow for or require a progression or regression, respectively.

The different positions are outlined here:

Half kneeling: This position is best described as a mid-lunge resting position.

Fig. 7.36 Half-kneeling position, shown as half kneeling with OH band pull.

Tall kneeling: This position is on the knees with hips extended.

Fig. 7.37 Kneeling position, shown as kneeling with OH band pull.

Standing: This can be modified from a wider to narrower stance, reducing the base of support.

Fig. 7.38 Split stance.

Split stance: This is the position of having one foot in front of the other.
Single leg stance: On one foot.

Fig. 7.39 Single leg stance.

Some exercises may lend themselves to being performed in a sitting position. This is a position that is very specific to either the sport or the outcome of performing an exercise this way. We would not say we wouldn't use this position as some rehabilitation may require this as part of the process, or we may be focusing on a specific weakness as identified face-to-face.

## Horizontal

The bench has been discussed as one of the Big Three movements. However, we need to be able to progress and connect this movement within the sporting activity or situation. The following exercises are designed to move through the build, connect, perform systems continuum for the horizontal press.

## Bench

Setting up by lying on the bench, the bar should be level with the eyes. A slight curve in the lumbar spine to raise the chest height and reduce the distance for a full-depth bench to be achieved should be encouraged, although excessive arching in low-trained athletes is not advisable.

The athlete takes a grip that is comfortable to them around the shoulder-width distance. The bar is to be pulled out of the rack, with the aid of a spotter, to facilitate a constant scapular position and force the shoulders and back into the bench. Pause for two seconds and let the bar compress the support structures in the back and shoulders. You may see the bar drop up to as much as 3in if this pause is used.

Start the descent by bending the elbows, which should move at around a 45-degree angle until the bar is across the lower ribs. Those with longer arms should ensure the elbows do not drop below the height of the bench, as this will overload the anterior portion of the shoulder.

Start the ascent by pushing yourself away from the bar; this maintains the focus on keeping the back in contact with the bench. The bar will travel slightly towards the rack due to the elbows maintaining their position underneath the bar at all times.

**Table 7.7   Bench press game-changing scores.**

|  | Game-Changer Bench Scores |
|---|---|
| Adult male | 1.25–1.5 × BW |
| U18 male | 0.75–1.25 × BW |
| U15 male | 0.5–1.0 × BW |
| Adult female | 1.0 × BW |
| U18 female | 0.75 × BW |
| U15 female | 0.5 × BW |

## DB Press

The bench press is the gold standard in upper body horizontal push for strength development. More often than not the athlete will require unilateral strength application for the horizontal press, such as blocking or fending off an opponent. As a result, moving from the bench press with a barbell to the dumb-bell press is an excellent choice for ensuring functionality. This exercise bags more benefits. The bench can produce much bigger lifts due to the technique of ripping the bar apart, forcing the contribution of the triceps to the movement. In the DB press this is not possible as you will simply pull the dumb-bells apart and lose the form of the exercise. Instead, the DB press forces more stabilizing musculature to be involved; in giving away the maximum output possible we create extra stability in the shoulder joint when applying force. This move is important to combat and collision sports to provide shoulder health and reduce the likelihood of injury.

This exercise is performed lying on a bench and in a similar manner to the regular bench. The elbows should create a 45-degree angle between the arm and the torso, then the DBs are pushed to mid-chest level and returned to create the 45-degree angle once more.

Both DBs can be moved at the same time as in a traditional bench, or can be performed unilaterally either alternately or a set on one arm then a set on the other in the one-arm DB press, which again is further along the continuum.

## Press-up

The humble press-up should be incorporated into many people's programmes. The ability to perform a decent press-up in any shape is a must.

To perform the press-up, start with the hands just outside shoulder width with the fingers pointing forwards. This creates the correct angle for the elbows to track (45 degrees) during the descent phase. Bending the elbows will start this. A full press-up is counted when the elbows are level with the back of the ribs. Further than this, especially for the ectomorphs out there, can expose the anterior shoulder capsule to potential mechanisms for injury. At most, the athlete's nose will be two fist widths from the floor, if not closer. The torso and hips are held strongly and in alignment during the whole press-up.

Full press-ups require the legs to be straight and in alignment with the hips and shoulders.

Knee press-ups are the next step down. There should be a straight line between the knee, hip and shoulder for these to count.

Should the knee press-up be too hard, do press-ups on a raised bench and gradually lower yourself to the floor once you have

**Table 7.8  Press-up game-changing scores.**

|  | Game-Changer Press Scores (@25bpm) |
|---|---|
| Adult male | 42+ |
| U18 male | 35 |
| U15 male | 25 |
| Adult female | 27 |
| U18 female | 20 |
| U15 female | 12 |

earned the right to progress the exercise's difficulty.

## Standing Horizontal Press

The standing horizontal press is one that often doesn't receive attention or is only performed on cable machines. Indeed, it is easier to perform with cables and provides direction of work that can work specific patterns, and we do use these in functional training programmes and develop them into split stance and single leg stance exercises in the cables; however we like to develop quickly into the standing horizontal press and use bands and free weights as the athletes are going to be using this skill against opponents who may not follow the rules. The standing horizontal press with a free weight can start with DBs or medicine balls (MB) and increase in weight. This main issue with this exercise is that the load typically cannot be high due to gravity pulling it down, making it more difficult to control the further it is pressed from the body. Again, this can be progressed with load and/or through the use of resistance bands as distractions or as the load itself. They can be performed together, singly and alternately.

Various heights and actions can be used in the horizontal press and should be explored. Two such positions are from the hip and from the chest. These alter the contributing muscles but can each be related to sporting actions.

## Horizontal Pull

The row is a simple exercise that can be complicated by over-thinking the exercise. As with the bench press, there is an optimal range in which to row through. In short, that is so the shoulder is not overextended. To do this the action of the row should not pass the athlete's obliques. This will ensure that the elbow is not too far behind the athlete, which would compromise stability at the shoulder, and also keeps within a strong mid-range that is useful in sporting scenarios such as lifting an opponent's leg in a rugby tackle, ripping a ball, or grappling with an opponent. There are many row variations, but we like to keep it simple and effective with a few exercises that are enhanced through variations to grip and/or stance.

# Row Variations

## BB Row

The BB row is a fantastic way to balance the overpowered upper body horizontal push athlete. The best part of this exercise is its capacity to actually increase bench press ability indirectly.

The bar is gripped (see below for variations) and the spine is rocked over to parallel with the ground with the feet in the required stance (also see below). The arms are long and hanging under load. The arms and upper back then work to draw the bar upwards towards the lower ribcage. Once here they extend again to return the bar to the hanging position.

# Grip Variations

## Over hand

The over hand grip is a standard in most barbell rows. Both palms are facing the rear, thumbs inside the hands, which is termed a pronated grip.

## Under hand

The under hand version is the reverse in which the palms are facing forwards in a supinated grip and the thumbs are pointing to the outside.

## Over-Under Hand

This grip is great to prevent the rolling of the bar out of your grip as typically occurs with the previous two grips, especially at higher loads. This is due the rotational forces acting in the opposite directions to one another in each hand. For each set alternate the over and under hand positions to prevent compensation patterns arising.

# Stance variations

## Standard

Feet shoulder-width apart, level with one another.

## Offset Step

This is similar to a jerk stance. One foot is one-third of a step in front of the hips, the other two-thirds back. This arrangement can alternate between sets or workouts.

## Single Leg

The athlete stands on one leg, as long as they can maintain hip level and are balanced. If the hips do offset, internally rotate the foot that is off the ground to bring the hips back towards the required position.

## DB Rows

Using dumb-bells to perform the row is great for increasing shoulder stability. They can be performed together, alternately or completed as one side and then the other (one-arm DB row). Again, the DB is drawn to the rib level so as to not compromise the shoulder.

Fig. 7.40 Dumb-bell (DB) single arm row.

## Chest to Bar (CTB)

The CTB exercise is an easy to step up and develop exercise. The squat rack pins are set to lower rib height as a starting point for this exercise. The athlete hangs with straight arms from the bar and keeps the shoulder, hip and knee in alignment. The athlete then aims to bring the chest up to the bar and then lowers him or herself again to complete the repetition.

To increase the difficulty, in the first instance the pins should be dropped lower one hole at a time, lowering the body into a more horizontal position. Once the height of the pins reaches a level equal to the length of the athlete's arms, you can add a block under the feet and go up a hole to keep the horizontal action and continue to add a block to the feet

Fig. 7.41 Chest to bar (CTB), shown on a suspension training system.

to invert the athlete. Alternatively, put the feet up on a bench, reset the pins to a horizontal position and drop a hole again. The grip can be changed to alter the focus and difficulty of the exercise; again using ropes, loops and towels can all add a different element to this exercise.

Depending on the weight of the athlete and the rack, it is sometimes advisable to have the torso inside the rack; however some racks allow for the feet to be wedged into the corners to prevent slipping.

## Suspension Training Aid

One of the staples of suspension training rigs is the suspended supine row, or what we call chest to bar. This exercise can be performed following the same guidelines as above and can be progressed through the angle of pull and by moving to single-arm exercises. Using a suspension training device adds a stability element into the exercise. Again, to regress the exercise start higher and build towards a more horizontal position. Adding blocks or a bench under the athlete's feet can also allow for continued development of difficulty in this exercise. Moving into the one-arm variants creates more instability and can be loaded by racking, or holding a kettlebell high on the chest. This exercise moves nicely into the suspended one-arm archer pull outlined within the rotation exercises section.

## Vertical Push or Overhead Presses

Many exercises have different names around the world. Here we look at exercises involving the vertical press, that is lifting a load from the shoulders or front position to overhead. The following exercises in BB form can be performed from the shoulders, behind the head, or from the chest in a front squat racked position. Both positions have their own limitations in the required head movement to lift

the bar straight up. The rear position requires adequate flexibility in the shoulders to grip and be strong enough to push in this position. The front racked position requires the head to move backwards to keep the bar from hitting the chin.

If you lack mobility, develop this by performing the front racked grip versions and pair with a shoulder mobility exercise such as wall slides. Don't be too proud to drop the load down too; you can advance your strength development by going back and getting it right.

## Military Press

We perform the military press with the rule that the bar comes to a level between chin and ear lobe height. By not allowing the bar to rest we maintain tension within the muscle to increase the muscle-building stimulus.

The bar is racked in the starting position, either on the shoulders or in the front racked position. The arms are bent. To initiate the lift the bar is pushed straight up through the contraction of the shoulder musculature. The torso is under tension and the legs are locked, not adding to the movement, until the arms are locked with the bar positioned above the crown of the head. It is then lowered under control to the start position to complete the rep.

In the military press you must be strict (like a drill sergeant) in not bouncing to get the bar moving. The movement is controlled, both in extending the arms and in lowering the bar.

## DB Military Press

To be more functional and add in a greater stability factor, DBs can be used. They also allow for those who are struggling to get the range of motion from the shoulders' action by allowing the movement to occur midway between the two BB positions. The actions

*Fig. 7.42   Dumb-bell (DB) military press start and finish positions.*

alternating arms or as a unilateral set. The DB is held in the start position with the opposite hand racking the DB similarly or hanging loosely if performed unilaterally. The action of the military press is performed, although there will be a likelihood of the shoulders adding to the movement and the working side rising to generate additional drive into the movement. Control the load throughout the exercise and back to the starting position.

## Push Press

The push press is a way of moving more load on the bar in a similar action, except this time the legs are allowed to be involved. It is easiest to perform this exercise from the front racked position and has better carry-over into the power and Olympic lifts. The upper body action is the same as the military press, but the athlete is allowed to dip with the legs and add momentum to the bar before the lift is essentially started. The athlete will select the required depth to add to the bar momentum naturally through trial and error. This is a necessary learning experience and the athlete should be allowed to experiment with different depths, especially if they 'miss' a lift because they have not developed enough momentum to start with.

The push press can develop into what Crossfit have popularized as a thruster. This is where the athlete performs a full depth front squat before driving the bar upwards in a seamless transition of front squat to overhead press.

are the same, and no leg drive is allowed within this lift.

## One-Arm Press

The one-arm press is a development of the DB military press. It can be performed with

## DB Push Press

As with the military press DB variation, this exercise follows suit. The upper body action is the same, the position that can be achieved in terms of shoulder orientation can be further back than the front racked position and the legs are again allowed to contribute to the DB momentums.

## Landmine Variations

The landmine exercise has received a massive amount of interest in recent years. Various complex and hybrid exercises have evolved. Below are the exercises we feel are functional and not as a hybrid for the sake of variation. Many landmine exercises can be performed two-handed or one-handed. Both grips have purpose in a functional exercise programme. Some of the exercises can use a double landmine action, where two bars are held in separate hands for the exercise and performed either alternately or together.

As a starting point, the end of a bar is placed in the landmine attachment, or sometimes the corner of a squat rack. A plate can be added to the opposite end and subsequent load is also placed here. The featured exercises all use an under-hand grip. This is where the bar is gripped from below, the bar resting in the skin web between the thumb and first finger, the fingers gripping to take control of the bar. If two-handed the hands can be separate grips in the same way as outlined above or overlapping where the upper hand's webbing is rested upon the lower hand and the fingers meet and overlap on the top of the bar.

Fig. 7.43   Landmine press exercise.

## Landmine Press

The press exercise involves the end of the bar starting on the shoulder and being pushed near vertically. For many holding the landmine position involves a slight forwards lean, which is accounted for in the vertical press by pressing in line with the body. This also accounts for the rotation of the bar in the landmine attachment. As previously stated, this can be performed with two independent bars simultaneously or alternately. To develop into a power exercise the legs can be added to increase momentum of the bar and create an explosive action.

## Landmine Rainbows

This requires the two-hand grip initially before significant strength levels are achieved. The start position here is with the slight forward lean into the bar, both hands gripping the bar overhead. The action begins by lowering the bar to just below shoulder height on one side, returning to the middle before repeating on the opposite side.

Fig. 7.44   Landmine 'rainbows'.

## Landmine Pivot Press

This is a one-handed exercise. In this action we start in a slight side-on position, taking the bar in the hand as that is away from the landmine attachment. The action involves producing force from the outside foot, driving through the hip, rotating the torso and extending through the loaded arm. The recoil is the reverse action. This exercise is great for transferring power into a punch, or lifting a player in a rugby lineout.

## Dips

A staple in the pressing department is the dip, a great pairing with the pull-up, chin-up or progressions thereof. It is an underrated exercise, most likely due to the difficulty some people associate with it. This exercise is of the same level of importance to the triceps and the upper arm and shoulder complex in general as the squat is to the quadriceps and hamstrings. However, it is not only the triceps group that gets worked during this exercise as larger muscles contribute significantly to the technique. The pectorals and teres groups contribute to the stability and force production capacity in this movement.

Dips can be performed on a bench as an entry-level dip; however this does not allow the muscles to perform the motor programme that is required during the parallel bar dips. As such, we recommend learning on the parallel bars; if it is too difficult to perform a body weight dip, there are regressions to reduce the loading. These include the use of looped exercise bands, or using a bench to place one foot on to support the weight of one leg, essentially reducing your bodyweight and making it a more achievable load.

The dip requires the body weight to be held forward of the shoulders, yet the arms are behind. This can be an issue for those with previous shoulder trauma or problems. If this exercise aggravates previous injuries consult an injury specialist before continuing with them. If in doubt as to whether you can perform them safely at body weight, start on a weighted dip machine and become comfortable performing 3 × 10 reps, 3 × 12, and then 3 × 14 before reducing the assistance and starting on 3 × 10 once again. Wean yourself from the machine as fast as possible without compromising on form.

Start by placing the hands on the bars in line with the hips, with bars that are around shoulder-width apart. The arms are straight and the body is held upright. You should aim to maintain this upright position throughout the exercise. The knees are bent and ankles crossed to concentrate the mass below the body. Lower the body down to a 90-degree elbow and maintain a strong shoulder position that is dependent on the athlete's shoulder range. Holding the upper arm parallel to the floor is adequate for this exercise, although those with longer limbs may stop short of this position because of the mechanical reasons outlined with the bench press and the compromising shoulder position. Push into the bar and return to the straight arms starting position.

## Vertical Pulls

### BB High Pull
The BB high pull, also known as the BB upright row, is an excellent shoulder and upper back exercise. A couple of grips are possible, shoulder width or narrow grip; where the bar is gripped with around a fist-width distance between the hands. These grips are both great at recruiting the upper trapezius muscles, although the narrow grip may have slightly more muscle fibre recruitment.

The bar starts hanging in front of the body with the arms straight. Palms face inwards, with the thumbs locking the bar by wrapping

them around it to meet the fingers. The bar is drawn upwards, close to the body, maintaining the palms inwards. The bar will reach just shy of the chin, and the elbows should remain higher than the wrists with the elbows moving sideways to achieve this. The forearms are above and follow the line of the bar. The bar is returned under control to the fully extended arm position to complete the rep.

If the movement is required to be a compound, whole body lift in a power development phase, then the lift can start from the UAP or hang position and eventually the floor (see explosive lifts section). When performing from the floor it is required to perform the explosive action and allow the bar to drop to the ground; this is because the load will typically be higher than what can be lowered under control following the explosive action. It is therefore suggested to add in the explosive BB high pull when there is appropriate flooring to do so.

### DB High Pull
When looking to progress the vertical pull and increase the stabilizers' role in the shoul-

Fig. 7.45   Dumb-bell (DB) high pull.

*Fig. 7.45  Dumb-bell (DB) high pull continued.*

ders during this exercise, the simple change can be to move to the DB high pull. The technique is the same, with the DBs starting in a hanging position a few inches away from one another, facing towards you. They are both simultaneously drawn upwards towards the chin and kept close to the body, then lowered under control.

The DB high pull is a good precursor to learning the one-arm snatch, and can be performed as a one-arm high pull to facilitate technique transfer further before moving into the one-arm snatch.

## One-Arm Snatch

The one-arm snatch exercise is moving the vertical pull exercise into the realms of power training. It can, however, be used throughout the strength-speed curve and can be loaded fairly heavily for power endurance training or lighter for explosive speed. It also requires considerable contribution from the stabilizers of the shoulder girdle and the rotator cuff on top of the agonistic actions required during the pull action of the lift. It also changes the vertical pull from low to high into a vertical

*Fig. 7.46 Dumb-bell (DB) one-arm snatch start- mid-finish positions.*

push and an agility exercise in which you are required to change direction under control very quickly and then control the weight while it is moving at its fastest. Thus the one-arm snatch is a versatile exercise to include within the vertical pull section of the training plans, and can be performed with kettlebells or dumb-bells.

Starting with the KB/DB hanging at knee height between the legs in a strong athletic stance (UAP), the athlete explodes upwards, pulling the KB/DB to chest height. At the moment of weightlessness the athlete drops under the weight into a deep squat, and extends the arm to a straight locked out position. To finish the move we require the athlete to stand up to full height with the load caught in the high position. When performing this exercise it is advised to keep the reps below eight to keep the quality and explosive nature and prevent bad form from fatigue.

## Pull-ups vs Chin-ups

Many people are in awe of others with the ability to perform pull-ups and chin-ups. It has been found in a survey of an American fitness club that around 70 per cent of their membership could not perform a single one of either. The participants in the survey were healthy gym-goers, not your average Joes, so this figure is most likely worse in the general public demographic. These exercises are great at developing upper body strength and build the athletic physique to which many aspire. This is because of the need to recruit massive amounts of muscle in order to perform each rep. These exercises are not just about biceps strength. They require adequate grip strength from the forearms, stabilizing efforts at the shoulder, the lats to add into the stability and also draw the humerus down, with the erectors and the gluteals providing anchorage points for the chain.

Many facilities provide a lat pull machine in place of the pull-up bar. Do not be fooled into thinking this is a suitable substitute to the humbling pull-up. The lat pull machine requires little gluteal and torso engagement because it fixes the lower body, concentrating the effort into the shoulder girdle. This exercise however does not recruit the stabilizers required for a pull up even though the shoulder action is essentially the same, you aren't controlling the body swing as it is fixed.

## What is the difference between a Pull-up and a Chin-up?

The difference between the two exercises is the grip on the bar. When performing a pull-up, the palms are facing away from the body. A chin-up is with the palms facing the body. These two positions change the involvement of primarily the biceps group. By having the palms facing you, the biceps are in a stronger pulling position and so many find this the easier option.

## Chin-ups

The bar is gripped at shoulder width or just inside, palms facing you. Legs are bent to concentrate the mass at the bottom of the pendulum, knees together and ankles crossed if desired. The torso is naturally tightened to control the swing of the lower body while the body is pulled upwards towards the bar. The chin should break the level of the bar in order for it to count as a solid repetition. Lower under control and minimize body swing.

## Pull-ups

The bar is gripped with a shoulder-width grip, or just outside, palms facing away. Again the legs are bent at the knees to concentrate the mass at the bottom of the body; if required, can be crossed to control any swinging that may occur. And the body is pulled upwards as in the chin-up, once again lowering under control.

**Table 7.9 Pull-ups/chin-ups game-changing scores.**

| | Game-Changer Pull-up/Chin-up Scores |
|---|---|
| Adult male | 20+ |
| U18 male | 15+ |
| U15 male | 10+ |
| Adult female | 10+ |
| U18 Female | 5+ |
| U15 female | 3–5 |

## One-Arm Pull-ups

Those who crave making the pull-up and chin-up harder (or who simply believe they may in the future have a need of pulling themselves and another to safety, Hollywood action movie style!) can move on to the one-arm pull/chin-up. The ability to control the swing becomes more challenging while hanging with only one hand. The action is the same as in the regular methods described above.

Pull/chin-ups and their one-arm equivalents can be developed by adding a dip belt with plates to increase the loading. They can also be made more challenging by changing the grip.

### DEVELOPING STRENGTH FOR A PULL-UP OR CHIN-UP

A negative pull/chin-up is when the athlete starts in the top position and then performs the eccentric action, or lowering portion of the exercise, in order to stimulate the strength in the musculature involved in the exercise.

### SETS AND REPS PROGRESSION

Week 1: Every workout 2 × 5–10 negatives
Week 2: 2 × 4+2 with <10sec rest between
Week 3: 3 × 5–10
Week 4: 3 × 4+4, Final session perform your first complete pull/chin-up

### DEVELOPING FROM ONE PULL/CHIN-UP

Using the same methods as the dips can aid the addition of extra repetitions. Reducing the load can aid the addition of extra repetitions. To do this, place a foot on a bench or chair to reduce the amount of body weight you are lifting, or better still, add an exercise band under the knees to maintain the correct position and therefore replicate the motor programme of the full pull-up.

Another approach that a group of colleagues tested was increasing the frequency of performing the lift. It is easier if you are able to use a pull-up bar daily. We used a challenge format to increase adherence to the method. Each day you had to perform a single set of pull-ups, each day aiming to add one or two to the total. We had a target of performing twenty within a month, starting from around eight or nine repetitions. This method allowed the group to reach the eighteen to twenty range within four weeks of four to six days of performing the test each week. The winner achieved the twenty reps in three weeks and four days. Not a bad gain in under a month of training!

## Grip Variations in Vertical Pulling Actions

To progress any of the above exercises we can alter the grips by many means. Here are a few variations I have used. These grips can be altered session to session, or can be mastered in turn over a period of time or sporadically thrown into the programmes to create chaos stimuli.

### Vari-grip

The variable grip is great to challenge the athlete's ability to perform the pull or chin-ups in less than perfect conditions. Some squat rack, cages and functional rigs have attachments that allow for parallel grip chin-ups as well as narrow and wide grip pull-ups. Having one hand in a different orientation or position creates a new technical challenge to overcome.

### Towel(s)

Hand towels can be wrapped around bars and racks to provide a challenging grip alternative. They can be knotted or left loose.

### Rope(s)

Rope attachments as lengths of rope, ropes with knots or even loops can provide versatile input into vertical pull exercises.

### Climbing Ball(s)

Climbing balls are special climbing wall attachments but are readily available on the internet. Designed to be gripped and hung, these grips really challenge your grip and forearm strength.

### Climbing Grips

In most indoor and outdoor climbing centres the walls are full of these attachments. Sometimes they are solid, sometimes they are able to spin to add an extra element. These attachments can also be used in some gyms also to create challenging grip strength and vertical pull progressions.

## Lunge Pattern

### Barbell Lunge

The barbell lunge is a great way of developing single leg strength, creating hypertrophy and coordinated movement. The bar can be placed in multiple positions to change the demands of the exercise or alter stresses on the body. Typically we will use either a back squat positioned bar or a front squat grip position.

Depending on the athlete, we will also use both forwards lunging action and reverse lunging actions. The front lunge creates an impact force and deceleration requirement of the front leg to overcome the force direction from the weights momentum, while the reverse lunge continuously loads the front leg with the load working vertically. If there are any injury concerns we would use the reverse lunge pattern in the first instance until the movement is fluid and can be controlled with

Fig. 7.47   Reverse lunge start-mid-finish positions.

*Fig. 7.47    Reverse lunge start-mid-finish positions continued.*

at least half the athlete's bodyweight before looking to include the standard lunge pattern into his or her programme.

## Offset Lunge

The offset lunge is a form of creating a steady distraction to the movement. By overloading the bar by 1.25, 2.5, or a maximum of 5kg if form is great and the athlete feels it is too light, we force the athlete to concentrate on maintaining positive form, focus on the key elements of the lifts, and can aid in developing neurological adaptations in imbalanced limbs. If looking for the correction of imbalances we would overload the weaker side with a plate, so that we create the stimuli in that limb in order to balance out the deficiency.

The main challenge comes in maintaining an upright torso. The athlete must work hard to prevent the natural sway and pull of the overloaded side.

## 3D Lunges

This is a dynamic lunging exercise in which the load is low but the intensity can be high. Start with a low tempo in order to perfect form and get comfortable with the movements.

The first is the lunge with lift in the sagittal plane. The bar or weighted object is gripped outside shoulder width, or if it is a medicine ball by the handles or sides. While standing the implement is held at roughly waist height. As the athlete lunges forwards, the implement is brought upwards with straight arms to reach the top at the same time as the athlete reaches the bottom portion of the lunge. As the athlete steps forwards out of the lunge, the implement is brought back to the starting position before the exercise is repeated with the opposite leg now taking the step. We normally perform this as a walking lunge with lift; however if you are short on space it is possible to perform each side for a number of reps in place.

The next movement is the lunge with rotation. We focus on this movement and rotation combination pattern because of our belief that we will encourage better patterning in actions such as walking, running and sprinting. As before, the lunge is performed with the implement starting at waist height. When the right foot is leading the athlete rotates the implement to the right; our cue is 'rotate over the lead leg'. This way we are accentuating and backing up the correct mechanics of the normal gait pattern.

The final movement is the lunge with side lean. This again is for the distraction of the normal pattern. Holding the implement overhead for the duration of this movement, the lunge pattern is completed. At the bottom of the lunge the athlete will have bent to the side of the lead leg with the weight overhead, as in Fig. 7.48.

## Compass or Clock Lunges

It is easiest to direct an athlete to perform this movement with a pre-taped floor with lines in the directions required. Eight strips of tape in a cross from north to south, east to west, and again at 45 degrees between each of these directions as shown below. Some pre-taped floors may use the clock face so that there are twelve directional lunges to be performed.

Fig. 7.48  3D lunges.

North and south lunges are performed as a regular or reverse lunge, east and west in the form of a goblet squat with the weight on the outside foot. The same rule applies with the directions in between; the weight is kept over the moving or outside leg, i.e. the weight is kept over the outside leg when in the NE/NW directional lunge or the SE/SW directional lunge.

In all lunges, depending on whether you are moving around the right- or left-hand side of the compass, the foot in the centre will remain there, facing forwards with the leg mostly straight. In the directions in which movement is forward in nature the weight is transferred forwards. In the directions to the back (right or left), the planted foot will be flat, and the outside foot is placed at 90 degrees across the tape, so that the athlete is required to 'sit back' into lunge. So when moving forwards, the foot that is moved/lifted to take the step will point to 12 o'clock. When moving backwards into SE/SW directions the foot will be angled perpendicularly to the direction of travel. The inside leg will receive various stretching effects during the exercise while the loaded leg will be strengthened by the need to control the weight shifting and the momentum of the weight transfer that will fire up the stabilizers in the hips and lower back.

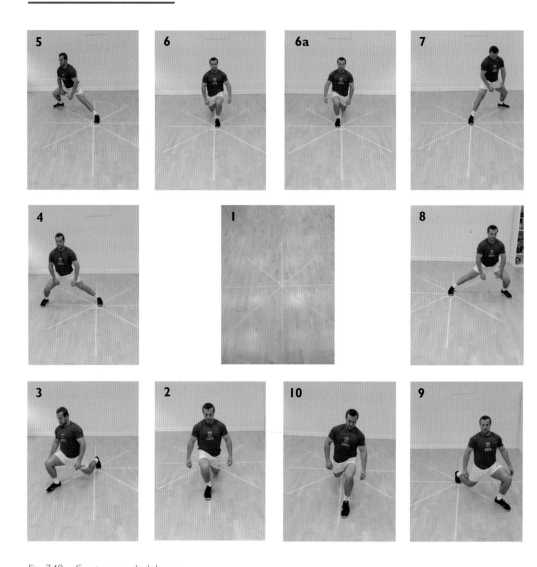

Fig. 7.49   Compass or clock lunges.

## Brace and Rotation Patterns

We group bracing and rotation patterns together in our programmes and interchange one for the other. It is important to develop the ability to brace and hold a position and then connect it with force manipulation, so alternating between these steadily builds the strength to hold a position but also to rotate while still being able to transfer effort through the torso.

### Squat to One-Arm Row

This exercise is designed to connect the lower body extension pattern with the upper body rowing action. This action is important in many sports, although this is not always realized. In grid iron or rugby, this exercise has crossover into the front-on tackle. The player will make the hit with the shoulder during the triple extension of the leg, and aim to lift one or both legs to prevent the attacker adding any more forward motion to the collision, the same in grappling sports. In basketball, how often do you see two players challenging for a low ball and the winner being the one who could rip the ball from low to high faster and stronger than the opponent, who is now sprawled on his or her front as the winner sets off on a lay-up.

The athlete starts in a standing position, facing the pulley and takes the handle in one hand. To get into the starting position the athlete allows the working arm to be extended and drops into a squatted position. Now as they stand they draw the handle into their lower rib. Be careful not to over-rotate in the squatted position as this may unbalance you and you will have a job recovering. If this happens, reset and go again.

## One-Leg Squat to One-Arm Row

The squat to one-arm can be progressed by performing on one leg. The athlete sets up on the right leg and holds the handle in the left hand. A single-leg squat is performed as the athlete extends the arm to the pulley. The squat would ideally be deep enough to almost cause the rear knee to touch the floor before the action is reversed and the handle drawn into the lower rib. Repeat on the other side for 3 × 10 repetitions. Increasing the load, altering the speed of the movement and also closing the eyes can aid in developing functional difficulty in these exercises.

## Lunge to One-Arm Rotational Row (One-Arm Two-Leg Rotational Row)

This total body exercise is a great connection exercise. This exercise works the whole body. On the field of play we perform movements that many whole body exercises just can't replicate. This exercise holds the key to making the connection between those whole body exercises that are great for developing athleticism and the agility work coaches perform in squad training sessions. The benefit in this exercise is the ability to load the cutting pattern and drive through the triple extension pattern in the opposite direction. I believe that this exercise will become a frontrunner in the prehab and rehab of knee injuries and have a direct impact on injury reduction in many field sports. The complex movement pattern allows for dynamic triple extension, loaded both eccentrically and concentrically, internal rotation at the hip and the transfer of power through a rotation in the torso.

The athlete needs to understand the action is replicating the explosive change of direction that can be used to exploit a defender's early commitment to a tackle or shadowing of a player. By being able to replicate this movement the change of direction ability will improve in most players and can be achieved at higher velocities due to the strength and neurological patterning of the motor programme.

To perform this move the athlete is required to stand sideways-on to the pulley system or band. The athlete takes the handle or band on their outside side (that is the one furthest from the attachment) and creates tension by drawing the hand to the hip. The athlete will already feel the pull of the load trying to cause torso rotation. With little displacement of the foot nearest to the attachment, the athlete rotates both feet 90 degrees as they descend into a short lunge facing the pulley. The shoulder is extended at the same time, reaching towards the pulley. Maintaining tension at the bottom of the movement, the athlete is required to reverse the actions in an explosive triple extension of the inside leg while 'snapping back' into the forward-facing stance and rowing the pulley back to the hip.

This exercise is ideal for slow eccentric loading in the first half of the exercise before the explosive action of the second half of the exercise. When performing this exercise 3 × 6–10 reps each side is adequate for developing performance delivering results.

## Suspended One-arm Archer Pulls

The archer pull is a single-arm exercise that works to stabilize the upper back and shoulder, rotate at the torso and finish up with the flexion of the elbow.

The athlete takes hold of the single handle of the suspension trainer. The feet are best placed in a narrow side-by-side stance facing the anchorage point. The athlete then lines up with the suspension trainer angle through the shoulders with the working arm straight, creating tension in the device.

The amount of torso stability depends on the line of pull during the exercise with the aim to eventually be working perpendicular to the floor but maintaining a straight body position, allowing the upper body to be rotated ~90 degrees.

The athlete then rotates the furthest shoulder towards the working hand and reaches up the trainer as far as they can, while the working arm performs a rowing action simultaneously. The finish position looks like the athlete has drawn back a bow and is ready to fire the arrow, hence the name. Under control the athlete returns to the starting position to reset and take another repetition.

## Anti-Rotation Press

The anti-rotation press is a staple favourite with our athletes. From equestrian riders and triathletes, to rugby players and powerlifters, there are ways of incorporating this action into their programmes and being functional with it. The movement requires the athlete to use a strong torso recruitment pattern yet requires stability in the torso and also the shoulder joint. In field sport athletes we perform this in primarily a half-kneeling or split stance. In riders we perform this on a gym ball, tall kneeling or quarter-squat position.

The athlete uses a rope attachment or a bar with the pulley attached at one end. Gripping at around shoulder width, the athlete starts by turning their hips in line with the line of pull. Depending on the athlete's mobility, this

*Fig. 7.50  Suspension trainer single arm archer pulls.*

may or may not come into their comfortable, strong range of motion. The head is held looking in the same direction as the hips, and the toes are pointed down this line in whichever stance the exercise is performed in. The first pull comes from the arm at the loose end of the rope or bar. The aim of this first pull is to get the other hand into a stronger position to perform the second movement. The first pull moves the hands from hip height to shoulder height. As the first pull is reaching its pinnacle, the athlete rotates the torso and drives the other hand in a shoulder-height, punch-like action. The reverse is controlled in a slow action before starting the movement again.

Variations: Tall kneeling, half-kneeling, GB seated, standing, split stance.

## Corkscrews

The corkscrew is a great rotation transfer and single leg balance combination move. The movement includes a one-leg half squat, a torso rotation and a diagonal cross body pull. It exaggerates a powerful first step action, or a speed skater's starting push off.

To perform this exercise the athlete stands side-on to the pulley (or band) with the foot nearest the pulley the supporting leg. The other is held off the floor. The athlete reaches across and takes the handle at below or equal to knee height. This will normally require a one-leg quarter-squat to achieve. Maintain tension in the pulley even at the bottom of the position. The athlete is now 'wound up' like a coiled spring and releases this by simultaneously extending the leg, rotating the shoulders and performing a cross-body, single-arm pull followed by an extension to create the furthest distance between the pulley anchorage point and the top of the movement. The difficult part comes in controlling the reverse of the movement to return to the starting position.

Note: if the athlete is having difficulty, regress this exercise by allowing the athlete to touch the toe of the non-supporting foot on the floor two feet behind. This normally creates enough stability to perform multiple reps of this exercise fairly confidently. If the athlete is still struggling you can perform a two-legged version but must develop into the one-leg

*Fig. 7.51*
*Corkscrew press*
*start and finish*
*positions.*

version as soon as possible to help with the transfer of power into performances.

## Wood Chops

The wood chop and reverse chop are diagonal exercises that require the torso to stabilize and transfer the effort through. The wood chop name comes from the axe-like chopping action in felling a tree. This exercise is useful to learn to transfer power through the torso but also has a crossover into sports where you may need to try and physically move an opponent in order to get into a superior position of attack; for example, getting past a lineman, movement within the key in basketball, and jockeying for position during a free kick in soccer. The action is to diagonally press the opponent so that he or she is placed into a weakened position.

The wood chop starts by setting the cable pulley high (above shoulder height) with the rope attachment. The rope attachment adds extra instability in the way it will move and reflects the fact an opponent may not move 'normally' against your resistance. Standing sideways on to the rope and taking it with a shoulder-width grip, the athlete stands tall, braces the mid-section and draws the rope in an arc down and around to the opposite hip. Slight shoulder rotation is allowed. The key here is not to flex the mid-section to create the power, it must come from the arms pulling and then pushing against the load. The movement is reversed before repeating again.

The reverse wood chop is the exact opposite action. The cable starts in a low position to allow the hands to start at hip height; the movement arc is up and around to slightly above the opposite shoulder. We work both of these exercises into the bracing patterns, sometimes working opposite patterns on the next workout or by focusing on proficiency over two or three weeks in one exercise before focusing on the opposite action.

## Standing Bar Rotations

As mentioned earlier, the way to injure the spine is to rotate through the lumbar region; with its smaller rotational ability it is prone to injury. It is important to understand the rotating through the thoracic spine concept before even attempting this exercise with a small unloaded bar.

To perform this movement the athlete stands with the bar racked across the back of the shoulders. As in the squat, the elbows are at 90 degrees or in a comfortable position close to this and are pushed back to create the shelf in which the bar sits. The athlete inhales deeply to fill the abdominal space and lungs and locks the abdominal musculature; transverse abdominis, rectus abdominis and obliques, and the lower back musculature; QLs, erector spinae and glutes. The shoulders are then rotated while the hips remain in the forward-faced position. This is then repeated side-to-side. The athlete is required to accelerate the bar into rotation and then decelerate the bar towards the end of the range.

# Brace

Bracing of the mid-section has received a lot of press over the last decade. With Pilates-style workouts on the rise it is necessary to sieve the better information from the chaff. There are different ways to explain how to stabilize the mid-section. The easiest way I can get a positive action from an athlete is to get them to replicate the defensive response to someone punching you in the stomach. The body naturally draws the abdominals and lower back muscles in to hold the organs in place and protect them from the impact as best they can.

This action causes the transverse abdominis (TA), which is like the body's own weight belt, to contract. Because it is wrapped from one side of the spine around the front and back onto the spine, this holds everything in place. The obliques contract, the rectus abdominis contracts, the QLs support the spine, the erector spinae hold the spine in alignment, the pelvic floor muscles lift. (Men, think of when someone walks in on you while you are urinating and you stop yourself, it feels like the muscles in your undercarriage lift a centimetre or so. This is your pelvic floor muscles working.) All these contractions occur to compress and solidify the mid-section to protect the organs and spine. This is also what is required when you are exercising or competing and require force transfer from the lower body to the upper body, or force reduction.

## Knee Drops

This is a great exercise to develop the ability to brace and have isolated lower body movements to complicate things. The athlete is required to brace the mid-section, and then allow both knees to drop from the sit-up starting position to the butterfly stretch position. This exercise forces the athletes with overpowered hip flexors to learn what it feels like to control the hip with the internal obliques, adductors and the transverse abdominis (TA). It also prevents the overpowered flexors from overloading the lumbar spine.

This exercise is not easy; if you find it so you are likely to be recruiting the hip flexors. A steady movement down and back up while maintaining the braced torso throughout multiple repetitions is required and can be straining.

This exercise progresses with the movement of individual legs to cause a different action on either side of the body within joining muscle groups.

## Lower Body Lying Rotations

The athlete lies on his or her back, with 90 degree hips and knees and arms outstretched.

Then allow both knees to drop to one side and aim to touch the floor before returning to the middle and repeating on the opposite side.

## Bear Crawls

There are many different crawl variations designed to stress the body in different ways, the bear crawl as we see it works the torso in a way that is simple and is easy to identify within many sports fields. The athlete starts in a four-point stance, that is with both hands on the floor. The knees and hips are at 90 degrees and the toes are also in contact with the floor. The opposite hand and foot moves at the same time in a pattern called the 'gait'. This replicates normal movement patterns in humans to move with the opposite arm working to counter the rotation forces of the leg. Any directions or course can be constructed to be performed in this position; however it is advised to also perform the more difficult pattern of reverse bear crawling. This has been found to challenge the athlete due to the lack of visual feedback and increased reliance on proprioceptive mechanisms, thus developing a stronger connection with proprioceptive components during motor patterns that may transfer into other activities.

## DSOHP

The athlete starts in a deep squatted position. The bar is racked as it would be in a back squat. Once at the bottom of the squat the athlete presses the bar up over the head, the athlete will normally experience a tightening of the erector spinae muscles and multifidus across the mid-back, especially after a number of reps have been performed. Each press is one rep and there is no change to the athlete's position in the deep squatted position throughout the set. Once the set is completed the athlete can then stand up.

## Plank Circuit

The plank position can be developed from the extended arms and knees press-up position, also seen as the hands and knees plank, to the full plank position of the elbows and hands and variations between. Once proficient in the hand and feet or elbow and feet position this can be integrated with the side plank, which again has various stages to build up to the elbow and feet variation. To perform the circuit the athlete starts by holding the plank position for the designated time. At the end of the time he or she transitions straight into the side plank on their left or right arm and holds for the duration again. At the end of this they move to the opposite side plank position. On completing this they return once again to the middle and hold the first plank again for the

same duration before resting. Typical times may involve fifteen seconds in each position and progress up to forty-five seconds in each position to work on strength endurance in the braced positions.

## Plank Push-ups

The plank push-up is a great transitioning exercise that builds upper body strength, coordination and torso strength development. The athlete starts in the arms extended press-up position. He or she then lifts one hand and places the elbow where the hand has just been, repeating this action on the opposite side so that they are now in a full plank position.

The first to be lifted is the one on the side that was lifted to initiate the exercise, e.g.

Fig. 7.52 Plank circuit positions.

right hand, right elbow, left-hand left elbow. Lift the right elbow and press up with the right hand, then repeat on the left to return to the extended press-up position.

This exercise can be performed continuously in the same rotation and then the reverse action for the second set, or it can be alternated on a time basis or after a set number of reps.

## BB Rollouts

The barbell rollout is an incredibly effective anterior abdominal exercise, but requires a strong all-round torso and stability within the shoulders. The exercise can be regressed by performing on a gym ball until the motor programme is ingrained. Moving from a large to a smaller gym ball is an appropriate progression in this exercise. To perform on the gym ball, start in a kneeling position and place the elbows at roughly the ten o'clock position in relation to looking at the ball from the side. Many athletes clasp their hands together and form a triangle or V shape with their arms. The weight is then moved into the ball and the elbows pushed away from the body, aiming to achieve a fully extended position and a

straight line between the knee, hip shoulder and elbow. Pulling the elbows back towards the body completes the repetition but can be the most difficult part of the exercise in both the gym ball and the BB versions.

To perform with a BB the bar should be loaded with small plates and secured with clips. Again start on the knees, this time with the arms straight and taking hold of the bar with a shoulder width grip. The arms maintain a fairly straight position as they are pushed forwards to allow the bar to roll away from the knees. This allows you to lower the torso towards the floor, aiming for a straight line between the knees, hip, shoulder and arms, before reversing the movement to return to the starting point.

Try not to arch the back; if this occurs you are going too far or need to regress to the GB version. Ideally the knee hip and shoulder will maintain the straight line for the duration of the exercise in both the down and upward phases. It can take time to achieve the target depth. Months of regularly challenging the motor programme will see steady development in this exercise. To progress this exercise you can in-

*Fig. 7.53 Barbell (BB) rollouts sequence.*

crease the load on the bar. This primarily affects the return phase of the exercise due to pulling a greater load back to the start position but this will provide benefit in torso bracing and performance. Eventually, some athletes are able to perform this exercise from standing and without letting the knees drop to the floor, which creates the longest kinetic chain and therefore the greatest rotational forces in the torso.

## Powerful Performance Phase – Special Exercises

### Upper Body – Vertical

#### Push Jerk
The push jerk is a continuation of the push press (which can also be used in the heavy vertical push position in the PP phase.) The bar starts in a front racked position, resting on the anterior deltoids. The elbows are high and the bar is gripped loosely with the fingers. The athlete dips and explodes upwards to create momentum. With the bar starting its ascent, the feet are slid, one forwards one-third step and the other backwards two-thirds of a step difference. The front knee is bent to around 60 degrees and the back creates roughly a 120-degree angle behind the knee. The hips and shoulders remain over the same point on the floor. The arms have extended and the bar is held in a locked out position above the head.

#### Loaded Pull-up/Chin-up
Weight is added to the athlete via a weighted vest, dipping belt or by grasping a DB between the knees. The pull-up/chin-up is performed as normal, although the load should reduce the number the athlete can achieve. This would be placed in the heavy vertical pull portion of the workout.

Fig. 7.54   Push jerk sequence.

## Med Ball Vertical Toss

This is to work the vertical push in a lightly resisted exercise to take advantage of the PAP response to the initial heavily loaded exercise. A medicine ball is cupped underneath with both hands at hip height. The athlete drops into the UAP, though greater leniency is encouraged for the torso angle, before explosively reversing the movement and throwing the arms skywards to release the ball. Care must be taken of others around you and to yourself when the MB is returning to the ground. *Do not* try to catch it!

## Med Ball Slam

The med ball slam starts overhead, with hands on the sides of the MB. The athlete will forcibly push the hips backwards and accelerate the shoulders and arms towards the ground. This is followed by the release of the MB to hit the ground from around waist height. Picking up the load to return to the start position is part of the exercise to start the coiling (like a spring) action of the muscles to stretch prior to the slam. This again would be a light vertical pull exercise to accompany the push press/jerk or weighted pull/chin-ups.

## Upper Body – Vertical

### Bench

The bench can be used as a heavy-loaded exercise followed by the kneeling chest pass as the light-loaded exercise.

### Kneeling Chest Throw/Power Pass

In the power pass, the athlete is required to start with both knees on the floor sat back on their heels with a 2–4kg medicine ball held two-handed at chest height. The athlete is instructed to use the hip thrust to generate force into the upper body and throw the ball as far as possible. If distance is limited,

place a target spot on the wall and aim to hit it powerfully (loud contact is a great cue for this) with each throw.

## Row Variations

All row variations can be heavily loaded to facilitate the heavy component of the horizontal pull section.

## Pendlay Row

This bent row variation is designed to create strict form in heavier lifts and powerful movement in lighter ones. The athlete's back must be parallel with the floor; the knees can be bent slightly to facilitate this. The bar starts from a dead weight position on the floor for each repetition. Gripping at shoulder width, the bar is pulled explosively to the lower ribs. The arms allow the bar to drop back to the floor and control the bounce of the bar. Reset the feet and body position before starting another repetition. If the bar is loaded lighter it is possible to return it to the floor quickly and under control without creating stressor forces in the back.

## Lower Body

### Triple Extensions

The athlete starts with the bar hanging loosely at hip height. The athlete takes up a UAP stance with the bar now resting at the lower thighs. From here there is an explosive hip thrust, knee and ankle extension that occurs simultaneously, and culminates in an aggressive shrug. With light loads it is normal for the athlete to leave the ground and this should be the intention. The athlete should rise vertically and land on the take-off points. Ensure the athlete does not over-arch or throw the shoulders back as this will cause him or her to travel in an unwanted direction (forwards or backwards) from the take-off. All power should be generating upward force.

*Fig. 7.55    Triple extensions start-mid-finish positions.*

## Clean

The clean is essentially a deadlift into a triple extension followed by catching the bar in the front squat position. The bar must remain close to the torso in the triple extension/second pull phase of the lift before the elbows 'snap' around and under to secure the bar. Elbows should aim to be higher than the bar to secure it in place. The bar should be gripped with a slightly less than shoulder-width grip throughout the lift. Often this will be used as a Power 1 exercise and loaded to >80% 1RM, or Power 2 if loaded between 40–60% 1RM.

The clean can be performed from the UAP also and this is known as the **hang clean**, which can be used as both a heavy- or light-loaded exercise in any of the positions in the lower body section. However, more often it will be as a Power 2 exercise or light exercise when loaded with less than 30% 1RM.

*NB. It is recommended you seek coaching in the Olympic lifts before inclusion in the programme. It is beyond the scope of this text to provide enough detail for the Olympic lifts to be performed the way our athletes would do in-house.*

## Snatch

The snatch would be used as the clean, in a Power 1 or 2 position. The grip is much wider, the bar is 'bounced' from the hip crease but maintains a close relationship to the body and the second pull involves 'jumping under the bar' to catch the bar in the overhead position. This exercise should only be included once supervised coaching has occurred for several weeks or even months. There are alternatives that will perform the required actions and create the desired effect for performance enhancement, so there is little need to get hung up on the Olympic lifts.

## Jump Squat

The jump squat is simple. Perform a back squat to the UAP depth and jump as high as possible while pulling the bar onto the shoulders. Try to jump as straight up as possible. This can be performed loaded or unloaded.

## Speed Deadlift

This is a light-loaded deadlift that allows the action to be completed quickly, creating a fast hip drive into the bar. The eccentric lowering can be slowed to increase the work into the hamstrings before the explosive hip drive is repeated. This can be in the Power 2 or light exercise position.

### Split Squat Jump

This is simply a stance variation to the jump squat; again this exercise can be loaded or unloaded. This is most frequently a light lower body action following the Power 2 exercise.

## Lunge to Rotation Row

### Heidens (Resisted/Non-Resisted)

Heidens are a great way to develop lateral explosive power required for stepping to beat defenders, making a cut or developing the ability to stop on the turn. The athlete starts on one foot and drops into a single-foot stance UAP in which the arms are swung to aid momentum in the direction of the jump. The simultaneous triple extension and diagonal drive of the arms in the direction of the jump creates the propulsion for the lateral jump. The athlete switches feet to land on the outside foot. This exercise can be resisted with bands or the use of a weight vest.

### Max height Jumps

An unloaded jump aiming for pure explosive power to reach the highest height. This would be a light-loaded exercise following the Power 2 position.

## Fx Metabolic sessions

The functional metabolic sessions use the principle called reverse periodization. It is a concept that turns traditional periodization on its head. Instead of building endurance and then getting quicker with that endurance we build playing speed and then endure that speed. It has worked well in both rowing (an endurance sport) and rugby union (intermittent team sport) squads we have been involved in. The benefit is that the athletes perform at a higher intensity earlier in the season while the opposition athletes play catch-up. At the end of the season most squads will reach similar standards; however we found that the recovery ability of reverse-periodized athletes is superior to traditionally periodized athletes and thus has the potential for reducing injury risk.

Traditional periodization develops the tank, the ability to cover a larger distance and then get quicker in doing so over a period of time. By doing it this way we teach the athletes to

Fig. 7.56   Heidens, lateral jumps starting on one leg and finishing on the other.

train the slower fibres while they reach capacity for distance before switching intensity into more focused sprint work. I believe that we can get better training adaptations of the fast fibres by training them earlier to perform at the required level and then make them more enduring of that speed. Surely an athlete that can perform 10 × 7s bursts at maximum intensity will end up winning the battle with an opponent who can go on for the whole game but can't keep pace those ten times? We use the following protocols and schemes to achieve these goals and produce physically rounded yet quick athletes in our programme.

## HIIT (High-Intensity Interval Training)

HIIT has gathered a lot of momentum in recent years. It is essentially repeated efforts over a short duration, interspersed with short rests for a number of sets with longer recovery times between the sets.

The pros of implementing HIIT protocols within your training, either on a separate day or a separate session (minimum of four hours post gym workout), allows you to concurrently train strength and power work from the gym, with the sport-specific work from the repeated bouts of effort.

Obviously, high-intensity sprints work on improving the sprinting ability of the athlete. This is one area where HIIT benefits. The way we explain the addition of this mode into your training is as follows:

You have a maximum speed that can be improved. As part of your maximum physical output you have a point at which you could continue running/cycling/rowing almost indefinitely (nutrition-dependent); this is termed the critical speed. Imagine this as a percentage of your maximum. As we said, your maximum increases and your critical speed will move up with that. Say, for argument's sake, that your critical speed is at 80 per cent of your maximum (eighty units). If you improve your maxi-

mum output from 100 units by 20 per cent to 120 units, 80 per cent of 120 is now your critical speed, or ninety-six units. You can now perform at a higher intensity, equivalent to 96 per cent of your previous maximum. Do note that this is purely an illustrative example.

Naturally the ability to work for longer at a higher intensity will obviously lead to better physical performance within a sporting situation.

The secondary benefit of this scheme is that the reduction in the rest periods increases the ability to recover aerobically more quickly, but this has a two-pronged effect. Obviously you are able to recover between bouts of intense work on the field, but this ability is a reflection of your aerobic capacity, so if recovery is improved, so is your aerobic capacity. Therefore you can perform endurance-type exercise at the same intensity for longer or at a higher intensity for the same time, both of which will improve performances in many sports.

In the protocols used in the functional training system whether on rowing machine, spin bike or on foot, all are able to be completed in short periods of time. We rotate different protocols throughout the cycles and they can be chopped and changed depending on the time constraints and focus on different speeds to induce a metabolic change.

The first protocol is a HIIT scheme that we have used in an array of sports and in different modes of locomotion, sometimes with a slight change of a variable.

In the first instance we start with four repetitions of sprints. These sprints are required to be all out efforts. After these sprints you rest for 20sec. It is so important to work maximally here to benefit from the HIIT sprint training.

NB: For HIIT to be as effective as possible some cardio work on top of it is required to benefit fully and achieve a positive response to this method of training. This may be in the form of the regular team sessions or fixtures of your given sport. If using this in personal pre-season training, also build in longer runs. HIIT works in intermittent sports and endurance sports when used as part of the endurance training scheme. If it was this simple to increase endurance marathon runners would solely use this method, and sprinters would be able to cover marathon distances easily, with good speed, which is not often the case, hence the aerobic work to complement the HIIT is a necessity for more endurance sports athletes.

## Differences between the Modes

Traditionally, we would use a 20m shuttle run. This will take less than 10sec. You then actively rest for 20sec. As previously mentioned, you would start with four sprints. Each week we would add a repetition until we have six sprints in each set. There are three sets in the HIIT workout. The between sets rest period starts with 5min. Once you have completed a

month of 3 × 6 sprints up to twice a week we would look to drop the rest period between sets by a minute per month down to 3min. Go below this level and we start stretching the recovery process to being in the area of not achieving enough recovery.

For the 3 × 6 sprints with 5min rest the workout lasts ~18min, 2min 40sec for each of the three sets, or 8min of HIIT work, plus 10min of between set rest. Add in a 10min warm-up, and 10min stretching and you have a workout that is effective in under 40min.

If you are using this method in cycling or rowing then we will perform this on the same equipment, either spin bike/turbo or on a rowing machine (or erg). However it is difficult to perform a shuttle in these modes and so we look to perform maximum efforts at low resistance for 10sec, resting for 20sec; the rest of the scheme works in the same way. We are looking for explosive max efforts for the 10sec. From experience, the reason we advise low resistances is due to the need to overcome the inertia of a standing start in both of these modes. We found it took around 4sec to get up to work speed, which caused undue fatigue and reduced the effort's intensity. For spin bike/turbo use low gears/

| Round 1 | Round 2 | Round 3 |
|---|---|---|
| 1 sprint ~10 seconds rest for 20 seconds | 4 sprints ~10 seconds duration followed by 20 seconds rest between each sprint | 4 sprints ~10 seconds duration followed by 20 seconds rest between each sprint |
| 1 sprint ~10 seconds rest for 20 seconds | | |
| 1 sprint ~10 seconds rest for 20 seconds | | |
| 1 sprint ~10 seconds | | |

Fig. 7.57  High-intensity interval training (HIIT).

resistance and for traditional Concept II rowing machines we advise levels 1–3.

Between rounds complete an activity for the period of 3 to 5min as described. This may include sports skill drills, mobility work or active resting by walking around.

## MAS Grid

If you are plateauing in the HIIT work or the competition demands are changing, you can move on to another conditioning system. This next system is ideal in heavy competition periods to increase your cruising speed, or the ground covered in a specific time. It has been documented previously as the MAS Grid

method (Maximum Aerobic Speed Grid). We have adapted it to be useful in individual and groups of athletes. It works on a percentage of your ability to cover distance in 15sec. This is tested by a simple distance in a set time test, normally 5 or 6min in the mode in which you will be training. The test requires the time to be longer than 3min so that you will settle into your critical speed but not cross into a higher anaerobically demanding intensity.

The grid can be on a field, artificial turf, hard court or a running track. Take the distance you completed in the 5 or 6min, divide either by the number of minutes and then again by four (for 15sec) or divide by the number of

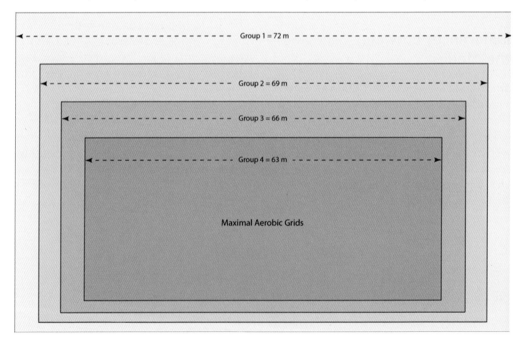

*Fig. 7.58  A maximal aerobic grid consists of rectangular grids, with the long sides equal to 100% MAS and the short sides 70% MAS. Each side takes 15sec to complete, with the full rectangle therefore taking 1min. The distances (long, horizontal sides: short vertical sides) for four theoretical groups are: Group 1 = 72m: 50m; Group 2 = 69m: 48m; Group 3 = 66m: 46m; Group 4 = 63m: 44m. Groups can start at different corners to allow for better spacing and less congestion. Nonetheless, all athletes hit a corner at the same time every fifteen seconds. A single conditioning coach can stand in the middle to ensure that the athletes make it to their corners at the same time, or, with multiple coaches, a coach can be stationed on each corner.*

seconds and multiply by fifteen. This figure is your 100 per cent MAS (Maximum Aerobic Speed). This is used to identify the working length of the grid. Seventy per cent of this is the resting distance.

*Example: Mark runs 1,500m in his distance test. This relates to a 15sec 100% MAS distance of 75m, the rest at 70% is a distance of 52.5m. Therefore Mark should create a grid/box that is 75m long by 52.5m wide.*

To complete the exercise, Mark starts by running the long side of the grid (75m). He has 15sec to make it from the first corner to the next. He tries to time it so that he makes it just in time, so he doesn't need to stop at each corner but just vary his speed. He then runs the short side (52.5m) at a slower pace, again to make the corner at 15sec, twice more completes the lap. Each lap will take 60sec.

The duration of the exercise starts at 6min and rises up to 8min over three weeks; when performed twice a week you can expect the participants' distance test to be bettered by an average of 8 per cent in most responders. (Some people have shown little or no response, which can be due to intrinsic motivation or injuries.)

If performed on a running track the markers should alternate between the long, work distances, and the short, rest distances; however it may not add up perfectly to a 400m distance and thus the above example would equate to three work and rest periods (totalling 382.5m), leaving 17.5m of track. In this instance we may look at pushing the rest distance up to 55 or 57.5m to close the gap and restart the lap. Four laps will equate to the total workout in this case. This will not affect the recovery to a significant degree.

# CHAPTER 8

# POST-WORKOUT

## Recovery Strategy

*Recovery is not just about doing enough to get your body back to pre-workout state, it is to get you beyond that!*

Would you be happy to train hard and have no gains over a year? Many people around the world do this and here is the reason why. If you only recover to the level you were at before the workout, you have not progressed, you have not developed. You may even ask why did you do the workout? We all train to get fitter, stronger, bigger and faster. To do that you must stress the body and the fitness component you wish to adapt, allow for it to surpass recovery and train again from this new baseline. Repeatedly doing so creates the development you are looking for. This is the basic theory of training, the GAS theory or super-compensation theory.

Train causing a fatiguing response. Take part in a recovery strategy (or not) and after a time you start allowing the body to gradually become bigger, faster or stronger. If you fail to train during the super-compensation period you will revert to the original baseline; if you train in the super-compensation period regularly and allow for adequate recovery you will improve performance in the gym sense. If you stress the body too far you will lead to exhaustion or over-training. Rest will allow you to regain the fitness but you may have time out of competition and training before

you get back up to the baseline before you over-trained.

What can be done to improve the recovery process so we get the super-compensation we need to improve our fitness? We can apply a simple strategy to help keep us on top of the recovery pathway once we have trained.

We have found that the Total Quality Recovery (TQR) score is an effective aid for the athletes in taking responsibility in their own recovery after sessions. It covers nutrition, hydration, active recovery and rest, and can be monitored by athlete and coach with a simple scoring system that takes a few days with which to get accustomed.

## Monitoring Recovery

### TQR (Total Quality Recovery) Points System

The TQR is a simple system by which you can quickly note where you are providing your body the best opportunity to recover from any training session. This can be noted down in your training diary once you have the points system ingrained in your mind or can be ticked off a list each day so you can keep track of the points. The aim is to get up to twenty points from your actions throughout the twenty-four hours post-training. The scale starts at six points being no recovery achieved.

Fifteen points can be achieved by eating breakfast, lunch, dinner, a snack or two between meals to keep the nutrients flowing, keeping hydrated during exercise and throughout the day, having a good night's sleep and stretching the muscles after a session.

**Table 8.1   The total quality recovery (TQR) points system.**

| Recovery Strategy (Possible points) | | MON | TUES | WEDS | THURS | FRI | SAT | SUN |
|---|---|---|---|---|---|---|---|---|
| **Nutrition and Hydration (10)** | | | | | | | | |
| Breakfast | 1 | | | | | | | |
| Lunch | 2 | | | | | | | |
| Dinner | 2 | | | | | | | |
| Pre-workout snack | 1 | | | | | | | |
| Post-workout snack | 2 | | | | | | | |
| Hydration daily (clear/light urine) | 1 | | | | | | | |
| Hydration post | 1 | | | | | | | |
| **Sleep (4)** | | | | | | | | |
| Good night of quality sleep (8hrs+) | 3 | | | | | | | |
| Daily nap (20–60min) | 1 | | | | | | | |
| **Relaxation (3)** | | | | | | | | |
| Mental and physical relaxation (post-workout) | 2 | | | | | | | |
| General relaxed state daily | 1 | | | | | | | |
| **Stretching/Cool Down (3)** | | | | | | | | |
| Proper cool down after session | 2 | | | | | | | |
| Additional stretching of all major groups | 1 | | | | | | | |
| **Total Score** | | | | | | | | |

1. **Nutrition** (Max total of 10 points)
   Breakfast – 1 point
   Lunch – 2 points
   Dinner – 2 points
   Snacks between meals – 1 point
   Carbohydrate snack for reloading post-workout – 2 points
   Adequate hydration – throughout the day (clear or light-coloured urine) – 1 point
   During/post-workout (clear or light coloured urine) – 1 point

2. **Sleep and Rest** (Max total 4 points)
   Good night of quality sleep (8hrs+) – 3 points
   Daily nap (20–60min) – 1 point
   (Quality of sleep is measured by individual perception. Naps during the day should be short, too long will leave you feeling sluggish)

3. **Relaxation and Emotional Support** (Max total 3 points)
   Full mental/muscular relaxation ASAP after workout – 2 points
   Maintaining a relaxed state throughout the day – 1 point

4. **Stretching and Cool Down** (Max total 3 points)
   Proper cool down after each session – 2 points
   Stretching all exercised muscle groups – 1 point

To help you achieve this we have provided you with a points check sheet, the muscular relaxation stretches routine, and some basics of nutrition to help guide you in your recovery.

## Post Workout Routine (10–15min)

For each stretch, hold for 6 to 10sec, then go further and repeat twice, a combined total of up to 30sec per stretch.

## Nutrition Basics

- Bulking 40% protein, 30–35% carbs, 25–30% fats
- Fat loss 20% carbs
- Every day

**Table 8.2   Post-workout routine adapted from Bob Anderson (2000) Stretching, Shelter Publications, CA.**

| Stretch | Description | Muscle group |
|---|---|---|
| **Lying butterfly** | Lie on back, soles of feet together, rock side to side, controlled breathing | Groin |
| **Knee lock** | In a sit-up position, wrap one leg across opposite knee and draw down to top leg side. | Gmed, TFL |
| **Head raise** | In sit up position, chin to chest | Trapezius |
| **Look left, look right** | As above though chin to shoulder | Trapezius, SCM |
| **Shoulder blade squeeze** | In sit-up position, hands linked behind head, squeeze shoulder blades together | Upper back |
| **Arch flattener** | In sit-up position, tighten glutes and abs, add in shoulder pinch, and finish with chin to chest | Lower/upper back |
| **Opposite pull** | In sit-up position, one arm by your side, other palm up above your head, reach in opposite directions | Shoulders and lats |
| **Whole body opposite** | Make your body as long as possible by stretching fingers and toes away from the body in a straight line | Anterior of the body |
| **Opposite arm to leg** | As above left arm, right leg or vice versa | Lats, obs |
| **Knee to chest** | Keep one leg on the ground, bring one knee to your chest | Hamstring/glute |
| **Mushroom** | Knees to chest, chin to chest | Lower and upper back |
| **Gravity-assisted groin stretch** | On back, feet off the floor knees half way to chest, allow gravity to aid the stretch | Groin |
| **Crucifix rot** | On back, arms outstretched, bring leg across (knee at 90°) to rotate torso and place thigh at 90° to the torso | Lower back, Gmed |
| **Back extension** | Lie on your front, push up, maintain contact with hips | Abdominals |
| **Hamstring doorway stretch** | Legs in the air, against a door frame, lower one leg to the floor, ensuring back posture is maintained and knees are straight | |
| **Chest doorway stretch** | Grip door frame at shoulder height, move beyond threshold | Pectorals |
| **Forearm flex/ extensors stretch** | Apply pressure when wrist is flexed/extended | Wrist flexors/ extensors |

# CHAPTER 9

# TRAINING PLANS

## Example of Scheduling for the Various Phases

The programme is flexible enough for extending periods of each of the four phases. If new to strength training you may spend up to double the time on each phase and look to peak only once in the first year, in Month 12. This is because your body will continue to adapt to the new stimulus of the programme and you are less likely to see performance plateaus in the first year. It is not unknown for an athlete to continue with the founda-tions programme for ten months and still be making gains.

As your body gets acclimatized to functional training you may start experiencing plateaus. To combat that this system changes the way in which the body is challenged every six to eight weeks. This way the body has to change how it adapts and you maintain performance enhancements month in, month out.

By following this programme, you could easily devote five years to this system and continue to see functional performance gains without having to resort to a 'trick' or 'trend'.

**Table 9.1 Example 12-month programmes for Novice and Intermediate performers within this programme.**

| Month | | | | | | | | | | | |
|---|---|---|---|---|---|---|---|---|---|---|---|
| 1 | 2 | 3 | 4 | 5 | 6 | 7 | 8 | 9 | 10 | 11 | 12 |
| Novice | | | | | | | | | | | |
| Fn | Fn | Fn | Fn | Fx | Fx | Fx | Fx/BBP | BBP | BBP | PP | PP |
| Intermediate (at least 12 months experience, preferably 24 months) | | | | | | | | | | | |
| Fn | Fn | Fx | Fx/BBP | BBP | PP | Fn | Fn | Fx | Fx/BP | BP | PP |

Fn: Foundations
Fx: Somatotype specific hypertrophy
BBP: Building balanced performers
PP: peak power performance

# TEMPLATES

## Foundations Strength Template

|  | **Workout A** | **Workout B** |
|---|---|---|
| **Big 3 strength section** |  |  |
| A1 | ***Back squat*** | ***Back squat*** |
| A2 | Mobility drill | Mobility drill |
| B1 | ***Bench*** | ***DL*** |
| B2 | Bent row | Pull-up |
| (B3) | Mobility drill | Dip |
| **Connection exercises (focus pattern)** |  |  |
| C1 (Squat/lunge) | Goblet squat | Compass lunges |
| C2 (Upper push) | Press-up | DB bench press |
| C3 (Upper pull) | CTB | One-arm row |
| C4 (Hinge) | Hip bridge | Glute–ham raise |
| C5 (Upper vertical push) | Half-kneeling landmine press | DB military press |
| C6 (Upper vertical pull) | BB high pull | Pull-up |
| C7 (Brace/rotate) | Plank circuit | Corkscrew |
| Met conditioning | HIIT 4 (5'REST) | HIIT 4 (5'REST) |

## Fx Mesotrophic template

| | Exercise | | Set 1 | Set 2 | Set 3 |
|---|---|---|---|---|---|
| **A1** | | *Target reps* | *8* | *5* | *10* |
| | | Load (kg) | | | |
| | | Completed reps | | | |
| **A2** | | ***Target Reps*** | *8* | *5* | *10* |
| | | Load (kg) | | | |
| | | Completed reps | | | |
| **B1** | | *Target reps* | *8* | *5* | *10* |
| | | Load (kg) | | | |
| | | Completed reps | | | |
| **B2** | | *Target reps* | *8* | *5* | *10* |
| | | Load (kg) | | | |
| | | Completed reps | | | |
| **C1** | | *Target reps* | *8* | *5* | *10* |
| | | Load (kg) | | | |
| | | Completed reps | | | |
| **C2** | | *Target reps* | *8* | *5* | *10* |
| | | Load (kg) | | | |
| | | Completed reps | | | |
| **C3** | | *Target reps* | *8* | *5* | *10* |
| | | Load (kg) | | | |
| | | Completed reps | | | |
| **Metabolic conditioning** | | | | | |

# Fx Ectotrophic template

|  | Exercise |  | Set 1 | Set 2 | Set 3 |
|---|---|---|---|---|---|
| **A1** |  | *Target reps* | *6* | *7* | *8* |
|  |  | Load (kg) |  |  |  |
|  |  | Completed reps |  |  |  |
| **A2** |  | *Target Reps* | *6* | *4* | *8* |
|  |  | Load (kg) |  |  |  |
|  |  | Completed reps |  |  |  |
|  |  |  |  |  |  |
| **B1** |  | *Target reps* | *6* | *4* | *8* |
|  |  | Load (kg) |  |  |  |
|  |  | Completed reps |  |  |  |
| **B2** |  | *Target reps* | *6* | *4* | *8* |
|  |  | Load (kg) |  |  |  |
|  |  | Completed reps |  |  |  |
|  |  |  |  |  |  |
| **C1** |  | *Target reps* | *6* | *4* | *8* |
|  |  | Load (kg) |  |  |  |
|  |  | Completed reps |  |  |  |
| **C2** |  | *Target reps* | *6* | *4* | *8* |
|  |  | Load (kg) |  |  |  |
|  |  | Completed reps |  |  |  |
| **C3** |  | *Target reps* | *6* | *4* | *8* |
|  |  | Load (kg) |  |  |  |
|  |  | Completed reps |  |  |  |
| **Metabolic conditioning** |  |  |  |  |  |

# Fx Endotrophic template – 10 reps

| | Exercise | Reps | | Set 1 | Set 2 | Set 3 |
|---|---|---|---|---|---|---|
| **A1** | | *10* | Load (kg) | | | |
| | | | Completed reps | | | |
| **A2** | | *10* | Load (kg) | | | |
| | | | Completed reps | | | |
| | | | | | | |
| **B1** | | *10* | Load (kg) | | | |
| | | | Completed reps | | | |
| **B2** | | *10* | Load (kg) | | | |
| | | | Completed reps | | | |
| | | | | | | |
| **C1** | | *10* | Load (kg) | | | |
| | | | Completed reps | | | |
| **C2** | | *10* | Load (kg) | | | |
| | | | Completed reps | | | |
| **C3** | | *10* | Load (kg) | | | |
| | | | Completed reps | | | |
| | | | | | | |
| **Metabolic conditioning** | | | | | | |

# Fx Endotrophic template – 12 reps

|  | Exercise | Reps |  | Set 1 | Set 2 | Set 3 |
|---|---|---|---|---|---|---|
| **A1** |  | *12* | Load (kg) |  |  |  |
|  |  |  | Completed reps |  |  |  |
| **A2** |  | *12* | Load (kg) |  |  |  |
|  |  |  | Completed reps |  |  |  |
|  |  |  |  |  |  |  |
| **B1** |  | *12* | Load (kg) |  |  |  |
|  |  |  | Completed reps |  |  |  |
| **B2** |  | *12* | Load (kg) |  |  |  |
|  |  |  | Completed reps |  |  |  |
|  |  |  |  |  |  |  |
| **C1** |  | *12* | Load (kg) |  |  |  |
|  |  |  | Completed reps |  |  |  |
| **C2** |  | *12* | Load (kg) |  |  |  |
|  |  |  | Completed reps |  |  |  |
| **C3** |  | *12* | Load (kg) |  |  |  |
|  |  |  | Completed reps |  |  |  |
|  |  |  |  |  |  |  |
| **Metabolic conditioning** |  |  |  |  |  |  |

## Fx Endotrophic template – 14 reps

|  | Exercise | Reps |  | Set 1 | Set 2 | Set 3 |
|---|---|---|---|---|---|---|
| **A1** |  | *14* | Load (kg) |  |  |  |
|  |  |  | Completed reps |  |  |  |
| **A2** |  | *14* | Load (kg) |  |  |  |
|  |  |  | Completed reps |  |  |  |
|  |  |  |  |  |  |  |
| **B1** |  | *12* | Load (kg) |  |  |  |
|  |  |  | Completed reps |  |  |  |
| **B2** |  | *12* | Load (kg) |  |  |  |
|  |  |  | Completed reps |  |  |  |
|  |  |  |  |  |  |  |
| **C1** |  | *12* | Load (kg) |  |  |  |
|  |  |  | Completed reps |  |  |  |
| **C2** |  | *12* | Load (kg) |  |  |  |
|  |  |  | Completed reps |  |  |  |
| **C3** |  | *12* | Load (kg) |  |  |  |
|  |  |  | Completed reps |  |  |  |
|  |  |  |  |  |  |  |
| **Metabolic conditioning** |  |  |  |  |  |  |

## BBP Template

| Workout – Squat | | | | | | | | | |
|---|---|---|---|---|---|---|---|---|---|
| | Exercise | Reps | Sets | Load | Set 1 | Set 2 | Set 3 | Set 4 | Set 5 |
| **A1** | Back squat | | | | | | | | |
| **A2** | | | | | | | | | |
| | | | | | | | | | |
| **B1** | | | | | | | | | |
| **B2** | | | | | | | | | |
| **(B3)** | | | | | | | | | |
| | | | | | | | | | |
| **C1 (C1)** | | | | | | | | | |
| **C2 (C2)** | | | | | | | | | |
| **C3 (C3)** | | | | | | | | | |
| **C4 (D1)** | | | | | | | | | |
| **C5 (D2)** | | | | | | | | | |
| | | | | | | | | | |
| **Metabolic conditioning** | | | | | | | | | |

## BBP Template

| | | | | | | | | | |
|---|---|---|---|---|---|---|---|---|---|
| | | | | **Workout – Deadlift** | | | | | |
| | **Exercise** | **Reps** | **Sets** | **Load** | **Set 1** | **Set 2** | **Set 3** | **Set 4** | **Set 5** |
| **A1** | Deadlift | | | | | | | | |
| **A2** | | | | | | | | | |
| | | | | | | | | | |
| **B1** | | | | | | | | | |
| **B2** | | | | | | | | | |
| **(B3)** | | | | | | | | | |
| | | | | | | | | | |
| **C1 (C1)** | | | | | | | | | |
| **C2 (C2)** | | | | | | | | | |
| **C3 (C3)** | | | | | | | | | |
| **C4 (D1)** | | | | | | | | | |
| **C5 (D2)** | | | | | | | | | |
| | | | | | | | | | |
| **Metabolic conditioning** | | | | | | | | | |

## BBP Template

| | Workout – Bench | | | | | | | | |
|---|---|---|---|---|---|---|---|---|---|
| | **Exercise** | **Reps** | **Sets** | **Load** | **Set 1** | **Set 2** | **Set 3** | **Set 4** | **Set 5** |
| **A1** | Bench | | | | | | | | |
| **A2** | | | | | | | | | |
| | | | | | | | | | |
| **B1** | Squat | | | | | | | | |
| **B2** | | | | | | | | | |
| **(B3)** | | | | | | | | | |
| | | | | | | | | | |
| **C1 (C1)** | | | | | | | | | |
| **C2 (C2)** | | | | | | | | | |
| **C3 (C3)** | | | | | | | | | |
| **C4 (D1)** | | | | | | | | | |
| **C5 (D2)** | | | | | | | | | |
| | | | | | | | | | |
| **Metabolic conditioning** | | | | | | | | | |

## PP Template

| Exercise Circuit 1 | Reps | Sets | Load | A Upper | B Lower |
|---|---|---|---|---|---|
| **POW1 – Heavy explosive power** | 3+3 30sec rest between 3s | 5 | 10RM | BB push press | BB high pull |
| **Heavy loaded (>90%1RM)** | 2–3 | 5 | 4RM | BB mil press | Deadlift |
| **POW2 – Optimal loaded power** | 8–10 | 5 | 30–60% of 1RM | BB push jerk | Hang clean |
| **Max speed – BW/low load** | 5–10 | 5 | BW–30% of of 1RM | Med ball wall throw | Box jumps |
| **Circuit 2** | **Reps** | **Sets** | **Load** | **Upper** | **Lower** |
| **POW1 – Heavy explosive power** | 3+3 30sec rest between 3s | 5 | 10%M | Bench | SL step-up |
| **Heavy loaded (>90%1RM)** | 2–3 | 5 | 4RM | One-arm DB bench press | Reverse lunge |
| **POW2 – Optimal loaded power** | 8–10 | 5 | 30–60% of 1RM | Half-kneeling cable press | DB triple ext |
| **Max speed – BW/low load exercise** | 5–10 | 5 | BW–30% of 1RM | One-arm med ball | Heiden |
| **Metabolic conditioning** | 6 | 3 | Max effort | HIIT sprints | HIIT sprints |

# Peak Power Upper and Lower Body Templates
## (separate training days for each)

| Exercise | Powerful Performer – Upper Body | | | | | | | |
|---|---|---|---|---|---|---|---|---|
| **Circuit I** | **Reps** | **Sets** | **Load** | **Set I** | **Set 2** | **Set 3** | **Set 4** | **Set 5** |
| **POWI – Heavy explosive power** | 3+3 | 5 | 10RM | | | | | |
| (30sec rest between first and second 3 reps) | | | | | | | | |
| **Heavy loaded (>90%IRM)** | 2–3 | 5 | 4RM | | | | | |
| **POW2 – Optimal loaded power** | 8–10 | 5 | 30–60% of IRM | | | | | |
| **Max speed – BW/ low load exercise** | 5–10 | 5 | BW–30% of IRM | | | | | |
| | | | | | | | | |
| **Circuit 2** | **Reps** | **Sets** | **Load** | **Set I** | **Set 2** | **Set 3** | **Set 4** | **Set 5** |
| **POWI – Heavy explosive power** | 3+3 | 5 | 10RM | | | | | |
| (30sec rest between first and second 3 reps) | | | | | | | | |
| **Heavy loaded (>90%IRM)** | 2–3 | 5 | 4RM | | | | | |
| **POW2 – Optimal loaded power** | 8–10 | 5 | 30–60% of IRM | | | | | |
| **Max speed – BW/ low load exercise** | 5–10 | 5 | BW–30% of IRM | | | | | |
| **Metabolic conditioning** | | | | | | | | |

| Exercise | Powerful Performer – Upper Body | | | | | | | |
|---|---|---|---|---|---|---|---|---|
| **Circuit I** | **Reps** | **Sets** | **Load** | **Set I** | **Set 2** | **Set 3** | **Set 4** | **Set 5** |
| **POW1 – Heavy explosive power** | 3+3 | 5 | IORM | | | | | |
| (30sec rest between first and second 3 reps) | | | | | | | | |
| **Heavy loaded (>90%IRM)** | 2–3 | 5 | 4RM | | | | | |
| **POW2 – Optimal loaded power** | 8–10 | 5 | 30–60% of IRM | | | | | |
| **Max speed – BW/ low load exercise** | 5–10 | 5 | BW–30% of IRM | | | | | |
| | | | | | | | | |
| **Circuit 2** | **Reps** | **Sets** | **Load** | **Set I** | **Set 2** | **Set 3** | **Set 4** | **Set 5** |
| **POW1 – Heavy explosive power** | 3+3 | 5 | IORM | | | | | |
| (30sec rest between first and second 3 reps) | | | | | | | | |
| **Heavy loaded (>90%IRM)** | 2–3 | 5 | 4RM | | | | | |
| **POW2 – Optimal loaded power** | 8–10 | 5 | 30–60% of IRM | | | | | |
| **Max speed – BW/ low load exercise** | 5–10 | 5 | BW–30% of IRM | | | | | |
| | | | | | | | | |
| **Metabolic conditioning** | | | | | | | | |

# REP MAX vs PERCENTAGE CALCULATOR

| Max Reps Completed Completed | % 1RM |
|:---:|:---:|
| 1 | 100 |
| 2 | 95 |
| 3 | 90 |
| 4 | 88 |
| 5 | 86 |
| 6 | 83 |
| 7 | 80 |
| 8 | 78 |
| 9 | 76 |
| 10 | 75 |

Calculated through the Brzychi (1993) method.

**Predicted 1RM =** $\dfrac{\textbf{Load Lifted}}{\textbf{1.0278-(.0278(number of reps completed))}}$

e.g. Maximum lift of 65kg a total of 6 reps

Predicted 1RM $= \dfrac{65kg}{1.0278-(.0278(6\ reps))}$

$= \dfrac{65kg}{1.0278-(.1668)}$

$= \dfrac{65kg}{0.861}$

Predicted 1RM $= 75.5kg$ or simply (65 divide 86) × 100.

# PPO FOR EXERCISES IN POWER

| Exercise | %IRM Range | Demographic | Supporting Authors |
|---|---|---|---|
| Jump squat | 0%<br>30<br>30–50 | M, Div I athletes<br>Male, athletic<br>Female, athletic | Cormie *et al*, 2007<br>Thomas *et al*, 2007<br>Thomas *et al*, 2007 |
| Squat | 56<br>50–70 | M, Div I athletes | Cormie *et al*, 2007<br>Siegel *et al*, 2003 |
| Power clean | 30*<br>80** | M, Div I athletes<br>M, Div I athletes | Cormie *et al*, 2007<br>Cormie *et al*, 2007 |
| Hang clean | 80 | Male, pro rugby players | Kilduff *et al*, 2007 |
| Bench | 65<br>40–60<br>30<br>30–50 | Male, pro rugby players<br><br><br>Male, athletic<br>Female, athletic | Kilduff *et al*, 2007<br>Siegel *et al*, 2002<br>Thomas *et al*, 2007<br>Thomas *et al*, 2007 |

*Greatest bar velocity **Peak Power Output

# GLOSSARY

**Abduction**   Lateral movement away from the midline of the trunk. Raising the arms or legs horizontally, as in a star jump.

**Adduction**   Movement medially toward the midline of the trunk. Lowering of the arms or legs.

**Agonist**   A muscle or group of muscles that is described as being primarily responsible for the resulting specific joint movement caused by contracting.

**Angle of pull**   The angle between the insertion of a muscle and the bone in which it inserts.

**Antagonist**   A muscle, or group of muscles, that opposes or works against the contraction of another muscle or group of muscles.

**Anterior**   The front of a person, organ or body part.

**Anterior pelvic tilt**   This is the action of the pelvis rocking forwards, the sacrum moves back and the lumbar curve increases. This occurs in quad-dominant athletes, where the quadriceps group are tight normally due to over-training and lack of hamstring training, this is commonly combined with tight hip flexors further increasing the problem.

Identifying whether or not you can include pelvic tilt to your body movement issues can be identified through a simple test. Stand with your back to the wall, feet about a foot away from the wall with knees slightly bent. Shoulders and hips should be in contact with the wall. Take a hand and try to fit it in the space of the lumbar spine. If you can't get your hand into the space, you have a posterior pelvic tilt to contend with. If you can fit a fist into the space you have an anteriorly tilted pelvis. If it is just a flat hand into the space you have non-significant tilt either way.

**Anteroposterior axis**   See sagittal axis.

**Balance**   The ability to control equilibrium in either or both static or dynamic state.

**Centre of Gravity**   A point in which the sum of the body's mass and weight is distributed evenly in all directions.

**Central nervous system (CNS)**   The cerebral cortex, basal ganglia, cerebellum, brain stem and spinal cord.

**Closed kinetic chain**   A movement sequence that begins with movement of a free body segment and finishes at a fixed segment. It also cannot be cycled, e.g. a dive in swimming starts with the arm swing and finishes with the foot extension, it cannot be repeated in a cyclical pattern without another action first occurring.

**Concentric contraction**   A contraction in which the muscle or group of muscles shorten and causes joint motion to occur.

**Depression**   Inferior movement of the shoulder girdle, which occurs in the movement of returning the shoulders following a shrugging action.

**Distal**   Furthermost portion of a limb, i.e. fingertips/toes, or furthest point from a reference or midline.

**Eccentric contraction**   A contraction in which the muscle or group of muscles are lengthening in order to control the action at the joint(s) the muscle crosses.

# GLOSSARY

**Elasticity**   The muscle's ability to return to its original length following contraction.

**Elevation**   Superior movement of the shoulder girdle. An example is shrugging the shoulders.

**Equilibrium**   State of zero acceleration in which there is no change in the speed or direction of the body.

**Eversion**   Turning the sole of the foot outward, collapsing the arch and/or weight bearing on the inside edge.

**Extension**   Straightening movement that results in the joint angle increasing, e.g. elbow action when performing the upward phase of a bench press.

**External rotation**   Rotary movement away from the mid-line of the body, occurs around the longitudinal axis of the bone.

**Fascia**   Fibrous membrane covering, supporting, connecting and separating muscles.

**First-class lever**   A lever in which the axis or fulcrum is between the force and the resistance. Knee extension is an example of a first-class lever.

**Flexion**   Decreasing the joint angle so that the bones will come together, e.g. in a squat the knee angle is decreased and the femur, tibia and fibular get closer to one another.

**Force**   Mass multiplied by acceleration (F=ma).

**Force Arm**   The perpendicular distance between the location of force application and the axis. The shortest distance between the axis of rotation and the action of the force.

**Friction**   Force that results from the resistance between two surfaces when at least one is moving.

**Frontal plane**   Plane that divides the body laterally from side to side, creating a front and back portion. Also known as the lateral plane or coronal plane.

**Golgi tendon organs (GTO)**   A proprioceptor, sensitive to both muscular tension and active contraction, found close to the muscle tendon junction within the tendon.

**Ground reaction force**   The force of the surface reacting to the force placed on it; the reaction force between the foot and the ground in running.

**Hamstrings**   The common name given to the group of muscles on the posterior thigh. This includes the biceps femoris, semitendinosus and semimembranosus.

**Horizontal abduction**   Movement of the humerus in the horizontal plane away from the mid-line of the body.

**Horizontal adduction**   Movement of the humerus in the horizontal plane towards the mid-line of the body.

**Inertia**   The resistance to action or a change of action, resistance to acceleration or deceleration. Inertia is the continuation of the current state an object is in, whether that is motionless or in motion.

**Innervation**   Supply of muscle and other body tissue with nerves.

**Insertion**   The distal attachment of a muscle to a bone, usually the most movable part.

**Internal rotation**   Rotary movement toward the midline of the body; occurs around the longitudinal axis of the bone.

**Inversion**   Turning of the sole inwards, in the action of rolling the ankle or walking on the outside edge of the foot.

**Isokinetic**   Type of dynamic exercise in which the speed (or velocity) of the movement is controlled during maximal concentric and/or eccentric contractions.

**Isometric contraction**   A contraction that results in little or no significant change in joint angle due to no significant change in muscle length.

**Kyphosis**   Increased anterior concavity of the normal thoracic curve. When in reference to the lumbar spine, the lack of a normal lordotic curve, which results in a flattened back, is known as lumbar kyphosis.

**Lateral axis** Axis that shares its orientation with the frontal plane of motion and runs side-to-side at a right angle to the sagittal plane of motion. Also known as the frontal or coronal axis.

**Lever** A rigid bar (bone) that moves around an axis.

**Ligament** A tough connective tissue that connects bone to bone to create stability.

**Mass** The amount of matter in a body.

**Movement phase** The action part of a skill, also referred to as the acceleration, action, motion or contact phase. The phase in which the summation of force is generated directly to the ball, sport or object.

**Muscle spindle** A proprioceptor sensitive to stretch and the rate of stretch that is concentrated in between the fibres in the muscle belly.

**Neuron** Nerve cell that is the basic unit of the nervous system that is relied on to generate and transmit impulses.

**Open kinetic chain** When the distal end of an extremity is not fixed to any surface, allowing one joint to move or function independently of movement at another joint in the extremity. For example, in a cricket bowl, the spin generated by the fingers is independent of the action at the elbow or shoulder.

**Origin** The proximal attachment of a muscle closest to the midline or centre of the body.

**Peripheral nervous system (PNS)** Portion of the nervous system that contains the sensory and motor divisions of all nerves throughout the body excluding those found within the CNS.

**Plane of motion** The imaginary two-dimensional surface through which a limb or body segment is moved. Likened to plane of glass passing through the body.

**Plantar Flexion** Extension movement of the ankle, resulting in the foot and or toes moving away from the body, e.g. tiptoeing.

**PAP – Post-activation potentiation** The level of muscle activity when following on from a stimulation inducing activity eg Heavy Squats or Short sprint.

**Posterior** The back portion of the body or segment.

**Posterior pelvic tilt** Posterior pelvic tilt occurs when the pelvis sits back, the sacrum in held forwards position while the iliac crest is drawn backwards. Often this is a sign that the hamstring group are tighter than they should be and the erector spinae group are weak.

**Pronation** Internally rotating the radius diagonally across the ulna, which results in the palms being faced down. Can also refer to the combination movement of eversion, abduction, and external rotation at the foot and ankle.

**Protraction** Forward movement of the shoulder girdle away from the spine results in the abduction of the scapula.

**Proximal** Nearest to the midline or point of reference.

**Quadriceps** The common name of the anterior thigh muscles containing rectus femoris, vastus medialis, vastus intermedius and Vastus lateralis.

**Reduction** Return of the spinal column to the anatomical position from lateral flexion; spine adduction.

**Retraction** Backward movement of the shoulder girdle toward the spine, adduction of the scapula.

**Rotation** Movement around the axis of a bone, such as turning inward, outwards, downward, upward of a bone.

**IGF-1** Insulin-like Growth Hormone Factor 1, increases growth in muscles when present; loading muscles with resistance can trigger an increase in production.

**Sagittal axis** The axis that has the same orientation as the sagittal plane of motion and runs from the front to the back at a right angle

# GLOSSARY

to the frontal plane of motion. Also known as the anteroposterior axis.

**Sagittal Plane**   Plane that bisects the body from front to back, dividing into left and right symmetrical halves. Also known as antero-posterior plane.

**Scoliosis**   Lateral curvature or sideward deviations of the spine.

**Second-class Lever**   A lever in which the resistance is between the axis (fulcrum) and the force. As in plantar flexion.

**Speed**   How fast an object is moving or the distance an object travels in a set time.

**Spin**   An accessory motion characterized by a single point of contact on a surface that rotates clockwise or anticlockwise with the surface.

**Spinal cord**   The common pathway between the CNS and the PNS.

**Spine (spineous process)**   Projection of bone typically from an irregular bone, such as the spine of scapula or spineous processes on vertebrae.

**Stability**   The resistance to change in the body's acceleration; a body's resistance to the change in equilibrium.

**Stabilizers**   Muscles that surround a joint or body part and contract to stabilize the area in order for another area or body part to move or produce a force.

**Supination**   Externally rotating the radius to where it lies in parallel to the ulna, which results in the palm up position of the forearm. As referred in the foot when the combination of inversion, internal rotation and adduction occur together.

**Synergist**   Muscles that assist in the action of the agonists but are not primarily respons-ible for the action, they assist the refinement of movements and eliminate unwanted actions.

**Tendon**   A strong fibrous connective tissue that connects muscle to bone.

**Third-class lever**   A lever in which the force is between the resistance and the axis

(fulcrum), as with the flexion of the elbow joint.

**Torque**   Moment of force. The turning effect of an eccentric force.

**Transverse plane**   Plane that divides the upper and lower halves of the body. Also known as the horizontal plane.

**Triple extension**   The triple extension is an important human movement for locomo-tion. It occurs in many actions we perform, e.g. walking, jogging, running, jumping, stand-ing, lunging, even crawling, and all other deriv-atives of lower-limb locomotion. Once the knee, hip and ankle are flexed, all three work in the triple extension pattern to produce the straightening of the leg for locomotion, whether that is unilateral or bilateral, single or both legs at once. Within this text, the triple extension is also an exercise that is primarily used in the early stages of learning the clean exercise, or to develop the second pull of the clean.

**Triple flexion**   Most people will be aware of the term triple extension but it is often forgotten that in order to produce triple extension those three joints – ankle, knee, hip – must all be placed into flexion first. In action triple flexion is the change from stand-ing straight to squatting, keeping the feet flat on the floor and the shoulders over the base of support.

**UAP**   The Universal Athletic Position is a position that coaches and athletes cannot hide from. It occurs in so many sports, in so many situations, that it is without doubt a key movement position that athletes and coaches must utilize in order to improve the crossover of training onto the sports field. Some call it the jump position, get ready position, hang start; whatever you term it, UAP covers the bases. Finding the position is simple, yet easier for some than others. If testing yourself, use a mirror or maybe record yourself to find it more accurately. However, it does not need to be replicated exactly as it is rarely identical in each sporting situation. If coaching or finding it with a training partner or athlete be aware that when you ask them to stop, it can take some time before they do and are now not in the same position. To find the position, perform a counter-movement jump, that is from a standing position drop and explode upwards. The position where you transition from lowering to exploding upwards is the UAP. Now try to drop down and stick in that position, use the video or training partner to identify if it is a similar depth. Repeat so that you become comfortable finding this position, that your body recognizes the process and actions required to replicate this position and that you can find it easily each time you are required. So essentially, the UAP is a position where there is slight triple flexion of the ankle, knee and hip, the spine is held neutral and the weight is distributed to the mid-foot to allow for an explosive triple extension of the ankle, knee and hip to exert the forces into the situation or scenario you are within.

**Velocity** Includes the direction and describes the rate of displacement of an object or body.

**Vertical Axis** Axis that runs straight down through the top of the head and spinal column and is at right angles to the transverse plane of motion. Also known as the longitudinal axis.

# BIBLIOGRAPHY

Anderson, B. (2000) *Stretching*, Shelter Publications, CA

Baker, D. (2003) 'Acute Effect of Alternate Heavy and Light Resistances on Power Output during Upper Body Complex Power Training', *Journal of Strength and Conditioning Research*, 17;3, pp.493–497

Baker, D. (2011) 'Recent Trends in High Intensity Aerobic Training for Field Sports', *UK Strength and Conditioning Association Journal*, 22

Brzychi, M. (1993) 'Strength Testing – Predicting a one repetition max from reps to fatigue', *JOPERD*, 69, pp.88–90

Cormie, P., McCauley, G.O., Triplett, N.T. & McBride, J.M. (2007) 'Optimal Loading for Maximal Power Output during Lower Body Resistance Exercises', *Med Sci Sports Exerc*, 39;2, pp.340–349

Kilduff, L.P., Bevan, H., Owen, N., Kingsley, M.I.L., Bunce, P., Bennett, M. & Cunningham, D. (2007) 'Optimal Loading for Peak Power Output during the Hang Clean in Professional Rugby Players', *International Journal of Sports Physiology Performance*, 2, pp.260–269.

Raske, A. (nordic circled A) and Norlin, R. (2002) 'Injury Incidence and Prevalence among Elite Weight and Powerlifters', *American Journal of Sports Medicine*, 30;2 pp.248–256.

Thomas, G.A., Kraemer, W.J., Spiering, B.A., Volek, J.S., Anderson, J.M. & Maresh, C.M. (2007) 'Maximal Power at different percentages of 1-RM', *Influence of Resistance and Gender*, 21;2

Meija, M., & Berardi, J. (2005) *The Complete Guide to Building Muscle the Natural Way*, Rodale International, London

Boyle, Mike (2004) *Functional Training for Sports, Human Kinetics*, Champaign, Illinois

Robertson, Mike, *The Single Leg Solution*, DVD + Manual, Mike Robertson Training Systems

McGill, Stuart (2007) *Ultimate Back Fitness and Performance*, Stuart McGill PHD (5th ED)

# INDEX

# INDEX